SCHOLASTIC

Teaching
Early Math Skills
With Favorite Picture Books

BY CONSTANCE J. LEUENBERGER

NEW YORK • TORONTO • LONDON • AUCKLAND • SYDNEY
MEXICO CITY • NEW DELHI • HONG KONG • BUENOS AIRES

Teaching Resources

To Todd, with love

ACKNOWLEDGMENTS

*Big thanks to my editor, Joan Novelli, who collaborated with me on this book.
Thanks also to the friendly ladies at the Oak Bluffs Library, who kept me in a steady supply
of books. As always, thanks to all my friends and family, who supported me all the way.*

Cover of COLOR ZOO by Lois Ehlert. Copyright © 1989 by Lois Ehlert. Published by HarperCollins Children's Books.

Cover of MISS SPIDER'S TEA PARTY by David Kirk. Copyright © 2004 by David Kirk. Reprinted by permission of Kirk and Callaway, LLC.

Cover of 12 WAYS TO GET TO 11. Reprinted with the permission of Simon & Schuster Books for Young Readers, an imprint of Simon & Schuster Children's Publishing Division from 12 WAYS TO GET TO 11 by Eve Merriam, illustrated by Bernie Karlin. Illustrations copyright © 1993 by Bernie Karlin.

"Elephant Probability" (page 75) is based on "Pottle's Probability" in *Meeting the Math Standards With Favorite Picture Books* by Bob Krech (Scholastic, 2002).

Edited by Joan Novelli
Cover and interior design by Kathy Massaro
Interior illustrations by Maxie Chambliss, James Graham Hale, and Cary Pillo

ISBN-13: 978-0-439-57219-4
ISBN-10: 0-439-57219-3

Contents

About This Book

STORY TIME IS MAGICAL. Many of us have fond memories of cuddling with our parents while reading a good book, or listening, captivated, to a favorite story in school. Children and books go together naturally, and bringing math into the picture book experience for children helps them feel more comfortable with the language of mathematics. The best predictor of overall school success is reading, so it makes sense to bring mathematical concepts into the literacy arena. The NCTM states that teachers "should plan lessons so that skills and concepts are taught not as isolated topics but rather as valued, connected, and useful parts of students' experiences." (NCTM, 2000) This book features carefully selected titles that will take your students on magical literary journeys, delighting them with the drama of a wonderful story, and immersing them in mathematical concepts as well.

How to Use the Book

Whether children are enjoying *The Rainbow Fish* (page 14) or *The Littlest Dinosaurs* (page 49), each featured title offers clear and meaningful connections to help you meet the goals of your math and language arts programs. The lessons are organized by content standards: Number and Operations, Patterns and Algebra, Geometry and Spatial Sense, Measurement, and Data Analysis and Probability. For each title, more specific connections to the standards are highlighted at the beginning of the lesson. Refer to this information as you select the lessons and activities that best support your math program. Here's an overview of what you'll find in the lessons for each title:

◎ **Book Summary:** Learn what makes each story special, and get an overview of key mathematical connections.

◎ **Meeting the Math Standards:** The activities for each featured title are aligned with the Standards for School Mathematics (NCTM, 2000) and the Curriculum Focal Points. (NCTM, 2006) For more information, see Meeting the Math Standards (page 5).

◎ **Math Talk:** "Throughout the early years, students should have daily opportunities to talk and write about mathematics." (NCTM, 2000) This section offers prompts for integrating "Math Talk" into "Before Reading" conversations about picture books. By incorporating mathematical discussions into daily language, including conversations about picture books, children naturally make that language part of their growing mathematical understandings. Because understanding vocabulary has a significant impact on a child's ability to understand the topic, this section also provides a road map for helping children understand the mathematical concepts in each lesson.

◎ **Book Talk:** "Inviting children to respond to their reading, valuing their responses, and offering interpretive questions to support further conversation ensures that children will continue to think about their reading in similarly complex ways." (Pinnell & Scharer,

2003) With this in mind, each book features ideas for discussions and questions for "After Reading" activities. Mathematical concepts are interwoven with important reading skills such as making connections to the text, rhyming, predicting, and recognizing features of the text.

◎ **Skill-Building Activities:** Each featured title is a springboard for activities that engage children in concrete mathematical experiences they will remember, while reinforcing essential literacy concepts. Your students will enjoy counting blueberries with the Caldecott Honor book *Blueberries for Sal* (page 7, making musical patterns in *Thump, Thump, Rat-a-Tat-Tat* (page 26), and graphing favorite things with *Honey, I Love* (page 68). Activities naturally incorporate other curriculum areas to deepen children's understandings and encourage connections. You'll find ideas for games, arts and crafts, bookmaking, dramatic experiences, take-home activities, and much more.

◎ **Book Links:** These suggestions offer opportunities to enrich each lesson with more math-rich read-alouds.

◎ **Ready-to-Use Reproducible Pages:** Templates, record sheets, patterns, and activity pages are designed to enhance each lesson and encourage independent learning.

Meeting the Math Standards

As you review the standards connections for each lesson, keep in mind that the NCTM Curriculum Focal Points provide further support for organizing math curriculum. The NCTM identified these focal points based on the areas of mathematics instruction that need the most emphasis at each grade level. For example, at the kindergarten level, math instruction focuses on number and operations, geometry and spatial sense, and measurement. Each focal point is important for further study of mathematics both inside and outside of school, uses the best practices to help children learn mathematics, and connects with what is taught in earlier and later grade levels. Beyond these curriculum focal points, each grade level has "connections to the focal points." These connections help to bring in other important areas of mathematics, including data analysis and probability, which children use in significant ways as they develop understandings in the focal areas. For specific information about the standards and focal points, go to www.nctm.org.

Connections to the Language Arts Standards

The featured titles and activities in this book are designed to support you in meeting the following language arts standards as outlined by Mid-continent Research for Education and Learning (McREL), an organization that collects and synthesizes national and state K–12 curriculum standards.

Reading

◆ Uses mental images based on pictures and print to aid in comprehension of text.

◆ Uses meaning clues to aid comprehension and make predictions about content.

◆ Understands level-appropriate sight words and vocabulary.

◆ Uses reading skills and strategies to understand a variety of familiar literary passages and texts.

◆ Knows setting, main characters, main events, sequence, and problems.

◆ Knows main idea or theme.

◆ Relates stories to personal experiences.

◆ Makes contributions in class and group discussions.

◆ Asks and responds to questions.

Writing

◆ Uses forms of emergent writing to represent ideas.

◆ Dictates stories, poems, and personal narratives.

◆ Uses emergent writing skills to write for a variety of purposes, and to write in a variety of forms.

◆ Uses writing and other methods to describe familiar persons, places, objects, or experiences.

◆ Writes in a variety of forms or genres and for different purposes.

◆ Generates questions about topics of personal interest.

Gavin is skip-counting by twos and fives.

Assessing Students' Learning

Depending on the children and the activity or project they are involved with, different types of assessment will be appropriate. Following are suggestions for use with the lessons in this book:

◎ **Rubrics and Checklists:** These assessment tools make it easy to document the behaviors children demonstrate during project work. For example, with the Nine Ways to Get to Eight Mini-Book (page 32), children might complete a simple self-assessment checklist. (See sample, right.)

◎ **Anecdotal Records:** Many of the activities in this book lend themselves well to anecdotal records. Here's an easy way to keep track of notes for each child: Write each child's name on a sticky note and transfer the class set to a file folder. (See sample, left.) As you observe children working, record names, along with comments and observations. With this system you'll easily be able to see which children you've included in the anecdotal records, and which still need your attention.

◎ **Portfolio Assessment:** Many of the lesson projects, such as Marching Band Patterns (page 27), are perfect as part of a portfolio. You may also document larger projects, such as Find the Size (page 55), with photographs of students' work.

Name _____ Date _____

How Did I Do?

Theme _____ Activity/Project _____

1. Color the face to show how you feel about your work.

   I used words or pictures to tell what I saw or did.

   I worked carefully.

2. These are the words or pictures I like best:
   _____
   _____

3. This is something I would like to do better next time:
   _____
   _____

Bibliography

Baroody, A. (2004). The role of psychological research in the development of early childhood mathematics standards. In D. H. Clements, J. Sarama and A. DiBiase (Eds.) *Engaging young children in mathematics: Standards for early childhood mathematics education* (pp. 149–172). Mahwah, N.J.: Lawrence Erlbaum Associates.

Kendall, J. S. and Marzano, R. J. (2004). *Content knowledge: A compendium of standards and benchmarks for K–12 education.* Aurora, CO: Mid-continent Research for Education and Learning. Online database: http://www.mcrel.org/standards-benchmarks.

McClain, K. and Cobb P. (1999). Supporting students' ways of reasoning about patterns and partitions. In J.V. Copley (Ed.) *Mathematics in the early years.* (pp. 112–118). Reston, VA: National Council of Teachers of Mathematics.

National Council of Teachers of Mathematics. (2006). *Curriculum focal points for prekindergarten through grade 8 mathematics.* Reston, VA: National Council of Teachers of Mathematics.

National Council of Teachers of Mathematics. (2000). *Principles and standards for school mathematics.* Reston, VA: National Council of Teachers of Mathematics.

Pinnell, G. S. and Scharer, P. L. (2003). *Teaching for comprehension in reading grades K–2: Strategies for helping children read with ease, confidence, and understanding.* New York, NY: Scholastic Inc.

Blueberries for Sal

by Robert McCloskey

◆

(VIKING, 1948)

In this Caldecott Honor book, Little Sal and her mother are picking blueberries. As Little Sal drops blueberries into her tin pail and counts the sounds they make—"kuplink, kuplank, kuplunk!"—she meanders away from her mother and ends up trailing a mother bear. At the same time, the bear cub absentmindedly begins trailing Sal's mother. A comedy of errors ensues as each little one follows the wrong mother.

Before Reading

Math is always more meaningful when connected to everyday life; therefore it is mathematically important that students see the connections between their own lives and the math concepts they're learning. Explain that examples of math are found everywhere, and adults often use math in their daily lives without even thinking about it. Ask children to think of a time they have used math in their daily life, and share times you regularly use math in yours. As you get ready to read aloud *Blueberries for Sal*, ask students to listen carefully to see if they can find examples of math in the story.

After Reading

Your students will delight in the antics of this book, as Little Sal and Little Bear follow the wrong mothers. Research supports facilitating making connections in children's reading because it is what good readers do, and because it is essential for comprehension. Encourage children to make their own connections to the text by relating what happens to their lives. Ask:

◎ How do you think Little Sal's mother felt when she discovered a bear instead of her child following her? (Repeat with Little Bear's mother.)

◎ How do you think Little Bear felt? (Repeat with Little Sal.)

◎ How would you feel if you discovered you were following a bear around instead of the person taking care of you? How do you think the bear might react?

Meeting the Math Standards

Number and Operations

◆ Computation

◆ Adding and subtracting

◆ Using objects to compute; using mental computation

Tip

▲▲▲▲▲▲

The small plastic baskets used for berries in most supermarkets work great for sorting activities and for use with activities such as Gone Blueberry Pickin'. Small pails are available from Oriental Trading Company (orientaltrading .com; 800-228-2269).

Gone Blueberry Pickin'

Invite students to go blueberry picking with this fun adding and counting activity that also works great as an independent math center activity. You will need several small pails (or baskets; see Tip, left) and dried beans painted blue to resemble blueberries. (Save the beans for use with other activities in this section.)

1. Label the front of each pail with a numeral (for younger children) or a number sentence such as 3 + 4 = ____ (for older children).

2. With students working in pairs, invite them to fill the pails with the correct number of blueberries, based on the numeral or number sentence. You might provide ten-frames for assistance with one-to-one correspondence and counting.

A Tremendous Mouthful!

Little Bear tastes a "tremendous mouthful" of blueberries from Little Sal's mother's pail. How much is a "tremendous mouthful"? Does it mean the same to everyone? In this activity, students experiment with "mouthfuls" as they estimate what a tremendous mouthful might mean to their math partner, and then find the difference between their estimate and their partner's.

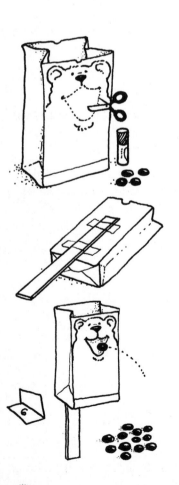

1. Enlarge the bear pattern (page 10) and give each child a copy. Invite children to color and cut out their bear and glue it to the front of a brown paper lunch sack, positioning the bear pattern as shown (left). Help children cut out an opening for the mouth of the bear, cutting through both the pattern and the paper bag. Have children tape a ruler (or other handle) to the back of the puppet.

2. Have children pair up. Give each pair some blueberries from Gone Blueberry Pickin' (above).

3. Have partners take turns secretly choosing a number (from 1–10, or any set you choose) and writing it on a sheet of paper. This number represents the number of blueberries in a mouthful for Little Bear. The child who chose the number holds up his or her Little Bear puppet, and the other child places blueberries in the bear's mouth, trying to match the partner's number.

4. Children count the blueberries in the bag to determine the difference between that and the number on the paper.

Storing Blueberries

The blueberries Sal and her mother picked were divided between canning for the winter, and feeding hungry tummies. In this activity children re-create their experience with math mats and blueberry counters to practice addition and subtraction skills.

1. Give each child a copy of the Storing Blueberries math mat (page 10). Each child will also need a handful of counters. The painted dried bean blueberries (page 8) work well.

2. Share a story problem based on the story—for example: "Little Sal's mom canned five blueberries, and Little Bear's mom stored four berries in her tummy!" As you share the story, use an overhead to model placement of the counters on the mat, placing five counters on the canning jar and four counters on the bear's tummy. Have children follow along using their own math mats. Then ask: "Who stored more? How many did they store all together? How many more berries did Little Sal's mom store than Little Bear's mom?" Write number sentences to go with each question (for example, 5 + 4 = 9) to show how many berries they stored all together.

3. Share new stories. Invite students to write number sentences to explain the berries on each math mat story.

"Kuplink, Kuplank, Kuplunk!"

As Little Sal picks berries, she drops them into her pail, "Kuplink, kuplank, kuplunk!" The sound of the berries hitting the bottom of the empty pail helps her count the berries. Students can strengthen their counting skills as well as their auditory discrimination skills with this berry-picking adventure.

1. Use colorful electrical tape to divide a cookie sheet into ten sections. Make two rows of five boxes each to create a ten-frame.

2. Turn the cookie sheet toward you, hiding it from children. Ask children to get ready to listen and count as you place "berries" (small magnets) in the "bucket." Place two or three magnets on the frame in order, one in the first box, one in the second, and so on. Invite children to listen to and count the sound of the magnets hitting the cookie sheet. Have students call out how many or hold up the number of fingers that match the number of magnets placed on the cookie sheet.

3. Show the cookie sheet to students, and have them count the magnets to check their responses. Repeat the activity for different numbers.

Storing Blueberries

A Tremendous Mouthful!

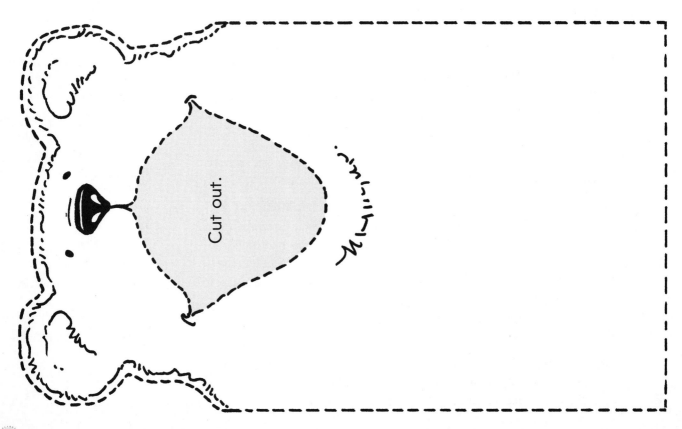

Cut out.

What Comes in 2's, 3's, & 4's?

by Suzanne Aker

◆◆

(SIMON AND SCHUSTER, 1990)

What do ears have in common with a bird's wings? They each come in sets of two. How about traffic signal lights and tricycle tires? They each come in sets of three, of course. Comparing sets of two, three, and four is the basis for a concept book that helps children use numbers to represent quantities and count objects in a set.

Before Reading

Recognizing "how many" in sets is a fundamental math skill. Beyond counting numbers in sets, children also need to be able to quickly recognize the number in a set without counting (such as how many legs on a table). This book is a great starting point for using sets, as it highlights groups of common objects that we see every day. Before reading the book, invite students to share what they know about sets. Encourage them to suggest ways they hear the word *sets* used in everyday life—for example, a class set of books, a chess set, or a set of building blocks. Explain that a set is a group of objects that are alike in some way.

After Reading

This book targets everyday math skills, emphasizing the ability to recognize "how many" in a set without counting. For example, some body parts, such as eyes, ears, and hands, come in twos. Things that come in sets of four are also easily recognizable (table legs, wheels on vehicles, and burners on a stove). Encourage students to identify the sets in the book. Discuss whether these sets are easily recognizable to students or not, and why. Ask:

◎ Do you automatically know there are four wheels on a car, or do you have to count? Why?

◎ Can you think of things that come in sets of other numbers? (for example, three wheels on a tricycle, five fingers on each hand, six legs on an insect, eight legs on a spider, and 12 eggs in a dozen)

Meeting the Math Standards

Number and Operations

◆ Recognizing the number of objects in sets

◆ Counting and connecting numerals to the quantities they represent

◆ Using physical models to represent numbers

Tip

▲▲▲▲▲▲

Explore differences between insects and spiders with these books:

Are You a Spider?
by Judy Allen
(Kingfisher, 2000)

Conversational text and large illustrations help answer the title question for young readers.

The Best Book of Bugs
by Claire Llewellyn
(Kingfisher, 2005)

This introduction to insects and spiders features eye-catching illustrations.

Children's Guide to Insects and Spiders
by Jinny Johnson
(Simon and Schuster, 1997)

Detailed illustrations highlight differences between insects and arachnids.

Tip

▲▲▲▲▲▲

To further reinforce the concept of sets, try lining up in different sets. As in *What Comes in 2's, 3's, & 4's?*, start out with common sets, then move into sets of other numbers—for example, "Wings on a bird come in sets of two. I'd like Gavin and Cole to line up in a set of two. Wheels on a tricycle come in sets of three. Sophie, Cheung, and Nora, let's line up in a set of three."

Creepy Crawly Counting

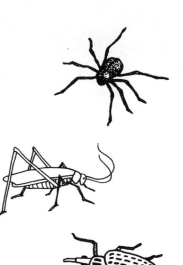

What do your students know about insects and spiders? Are there sets that go with each of these creatures? Help children identify the difference between an insect and a spider by counting their legs.

1. Share books about insects and spiders with children. (See Tip, left.)

2. Discuss that the number of legs on an insect or spider is a common group or set: Insects have six legs and spiders have eight. This is one way that we can tell the difference between spiders and insects.

3. When students are aware of the differences between insects and spiders, give each child a lump of clay, some wiggly eyes, and at least eight pipe cleaner pieces cut to approximately two inches each.

4. Invite students to create an insect or a spider with the correct number of legs. Their creation must be kept a secret!

5. When students' insects and spiders are complete, invite them to take turns sharing them with the class. Each student can call on classmates to guess the identity (insect or spider), using the number of legs as the determining factor.

Edible Domino Sets

For a great math snack that reinforces concepts of sets and matching numbers, as well as counting skills, try this yummy activity. You will need graham crackers, cream cheese, and raisins. Be sure to check in advance for allergies to any of these foods.

1. Spread cream cheese over the entire graham cracker.

2. Place raisins on one half of the cracker to resemble a domino.

3. When children are ready to eat, have them place the same number of raisins on the other half of the cracker.

4. To reinforce counting and number sense, invite children to add or take away (eat) raisins to make half the cracker show one more raisin than the other half, two less, and so on.

Collage Sets

Recognizing sets is the basis for addition and subtraction, and sets the stage for multiplication later on. Reinforce the concept of sets by having students create sets of their own.

1. Provide students with magazines, catalogs, scissors, drawing paper, and glue. Ask students to cut out pictures that show things that commonly come in sets—for example, a picture of twins for things that come in twos and a dozen eggs for things that come in twelves.

2. Have students make set collages. Depending on how many different examples of sets they find, have them divide the drawing paper into sections and label to represent the sets (twos, threes, fours, fives, sixes, and twelves). Then they can glue their pictures in the corresponding sections.

3. Display collages so that students can learn from one another other things that come in sets.

Book Links

Each of these books reinforces the concept of sets in a fun and different way.

Bat Jamboree
by Kathi Appelt
(William Morrow, 1996)

Each year 55 bats put on a bat jamboree. The grand finale is a bat pyramid, which is made with multiples of three.

Each Orange Had 8 Slices:
A Counting Book
by Paul Giganti, Jr.
(Greenwillow, 1992)

The possibilities are endless with this counting book, which focuses on sets of things.

More Than One
by Miriam Schlein
(Greenwillow, 1996)

A whale is one, and young readers discover that a pair of shoes can also be one, as well as a week of seven days and a baseball team with nine players.

Ten Black Dots
by Donald Crews
(HarperCollins, 1968)

Using rhymed text and counting, the author explores pictures that one to ten black dots can make.

The Rainbow Fish

by Marcus Pfister

◆◆

(NORTH-SOUTH BOOKS, 1992)

Meeting the Math Standards

Number and Operations

◆ Understanding relationships among numbers

◆ Understanding relationships between different operations, such as addition and subtraction

◆ Adding and subtracting

◆ Grouping objects in sets and sharing equally

In this ABBY winner (American Booksellers Book of the Year), Rainbow Fish finds happiness when he learns how to share his beautiful shiny scales with friends. Each time Rainbow Fish gives away another scale, there's a math experience in the making (subtracting one or counting back).

Before Reading

Math Talk

Show students the picture on the cover, pointing out the beautiful shiny scales on Rainbow Fish. Invite students to estimate how many shiny scales they think Rainbow Fish has. Ask: "Do you think Rainbow Fish has enough scales to share with others? How many scales do you think Rainbow Fish might share?"

After Reading

Book Talk

Rainbow Fish had a hard time deciding to share his beautiful scales, but when he did he felt much better, and gained some friends, too. To increase mathematical thinking and awareness, guide students in a math discussion about the meaning of addition and subtraction as it relates to sharing. Ask:

◎ If you share something, do you then have more or less of the item? (Let students use examples of sharing from their own lives to explain their thinking.)

◎ When something is shared, is it subtracted? Is it added? (Encourage students to explain their thinking, and then demonstrate this idea by inviting two students to come to the front of the class. Give one student six pencils; the other student has no pencils. Invite the class to brainstorm ways the students can share the pencils. Try out some of the ideas, and discuss the fact that as one student's set is being reduced (subtraction), the other student's set is being increased (addition).

Something's Fishy

These math mats make it swimmingly easy to understand addition and subtraction skills!

1. Give each child a copy of the fish bowl and counters (page 17). Invite children to color their fish counters.

2. Create addition and subtraction problems and stories for students to demonstrate on their mats. For example, you might say: "Four fish are swimming in the bowl. Two more come swimming along! How many fish are there all together?"

3. To reinforce learning at home, place students' math mats and fish counters in a zipper-close bag, along with a sheet of new problems to solve.

Fishing for Ten

Go fishing while using subtraction and critical-thinking skills in this math game.

1. For each pair of students, copy one fish bowl template and ten fish templates (page 17). Color the fish bowl a dark color, such as blue (or copy on dark paper), and color the fish bright colors. Laminate if you wish for durability.

2. Players begin by placing the ten fish on the fish bowl. Player 1 closes his or her eyes while player 2 places at least one of the fish under the bowl.

3. Player 1 then opens his or her eyes and determines how many fish are hidden under the bowl. As you observe students playing, encourage the use of math language, such as "I see six fish. I know there are ten fish total. Ten fish minus six fish equals four fish. That means there are four fish under the bowl!"

4. To reinforce learning at home, make extra sets of the game for children to play with their families and caregivers.

Book Links

Share these books with students to help support the concepts of dividing equally and subtracting:

The Doorbell Rang
by Pat Hutchins
(Greenwillow, 1986)

When Ma makes cookies for Victoria and Sam, she asks them to share them between themselves. As they begin to divide the cookies, the doorbell rings, and it continues ringing and ringing throughout the story, each time adding to the number of children sharing the cookies.

Gator Pie
by Louise Mathews
(Dodd, Mead, 1979)

Alvin and Alice are two alligators that find a pie. Their plan to share it equally changes each time another alligator arrives and demands some.

There Were Ten in the Bed
illustrated by Annie Kubler
(Child's Play, 2001)

This interactive book gives the reader an opportunity to roll a wheel and make a child "fall" out of the bed, reinforcing the concept of subtracting one in this classic counting rhyme.

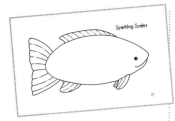

Tip

▲▲▲▲▲▲

To extend the game you can customize new dice that have more challenging math directions on them (+ 4 or – 5, for example).

Sparkling Scales

Students will love adding and subtracting jewels (fish scales) in this game of chance.

1. Customize a die by placing small, round stickers on each side and writing "+ 1," "+ 2," "+ 3," "– 1," "– 2," and "– 3" on them. Gather at least 40 colorful craft sequins or jewels. If these are not available, use buttons, pennies, or other counters. Make copies of the fish math mat (page 17).

2. Invite students to play the game in groups of two, three, or four players. Each group needs a handful of counters and a fish mat for each player.

3. Players take turns rolling the die and adding or subtracting the number of sequins indicated to their fish math mat. (If a player is to subtract sequins but doesn't have the number indicated, the next player goes.)

4. Each player takes five turns total. At the end of five turns, the player with the most scales wins! Or, for a collaborative version, players continue until they use all the jewels.

Tip

▲▲▲▲▲▲

To set this up as a center activity, make multiple copies of the fish templates (page 17), and substitute these for the crackers.

We're Going Crackers!

Draw children in to the concept of sharing equally as they experiment with division and equal amounts. You will need four empty bowls, a plate, and at least 20 fish crackers (or counters).

1. Arrange the plate and bowls where students can see them. Place four fish crackers on the plate.

2. Give each of four volunteers one of the bowls. Brainstorm with the class ways to divide the crackers equally among the four children—for example, they can "deal" the crackers one at a time to each person. Then have the four volunteers decide how they will equally divide the crackers and then do so.

3. Remove all crackers from the bowls and start again, this time placing eight fish crackers on the plate. Choose four new volunteers to divide the crackers equally among themselves.

4. Repeat with 12 fish crackers, then 16, 20, and so on, until you feel students understand the concept.

5. If desired, provide fresh fish crackers for students to eat. (Remind them not to eat the crackers that have been handled in the activity.)

Something's Fishy • Fishing for Ten

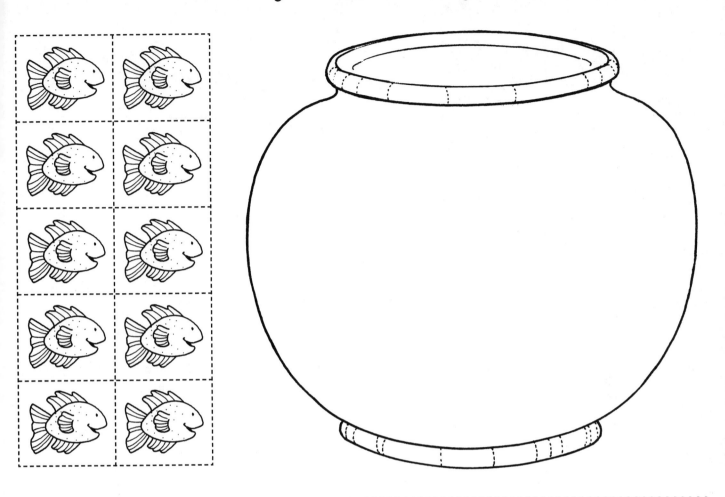

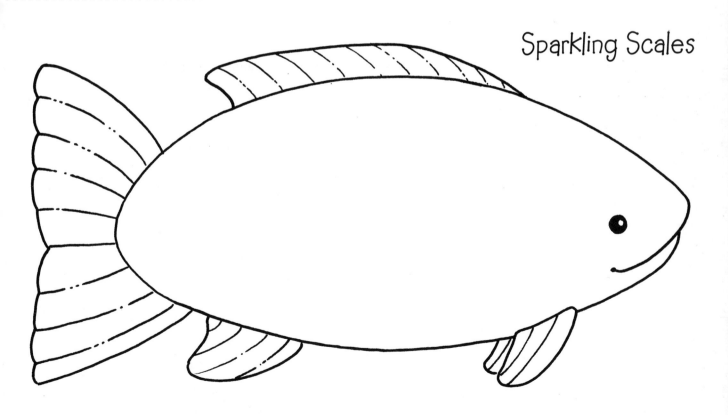

Sparkling Scales

Miss Spider's Tea Party

by David Kirk

❖❖

(SCHOLASTIC, 1994)

Meeting the Math Standards

Number and Operations

◆ Understanding the relationships among numbers

◆ Understanding the position of numbers

◆ Using models to understand place value and the base-ten system

◆ Adding and subtracting

Miss Spider is one lonely spider, and so invites some insects to tea. First she invites two timid beetles, and then three fireflies, and so on, as she counts to 12. Knowing spiders' reputation for eating their insect guests, the insects are fearful and decline the invitation. When Miss Spider dries a rain-soaked moth, the insects see that she is harmless, and soon her party is in full swing!

Before Reading

Math Talk

Although at first glance this book does not look like a counting book, it is. Show students the cover of *Miss Spider's Tea Party* and ask them if they think this book is a counting book. Explain that number words are part of the story, and that there isn't an actual numeral written on any page. As you read the story aloud, ask children to listen carefully for number words, holding up fingers to match the words they hear.

After Reading

Book Talk

Miss Spider's Tea Party is written in rhyme, which helps young readers predict text, making it easy for them to join in the reading fun. Try these activities to reinforce rhyming word patterns.

◎ Reread portions of the text, and encourage students to fill in missing words. Remind them to rely on the rhyme and context to decide which word fits best.

◎ To reinforce the concept of rhyme and spelling patterns, make lists of word families based on rhymes in the book. Start with word families such as *-at* (*cat, hat, bat, sat*), and work your way toward more challenging word families, such as *-ake* (*cake, make, take, bake*). Invite students to add new words to a list, and then read the words together.

Time for Tea

With its tea party theme, this activity reinforces basic addition and subtraction skills. You'll need an inexpensive set of play teacups and saucers (12 of each). You may also substitute paper cups for teacups and paper dessert-size plates for saucers.

1. Label the bottom of each teacup with a numeral from 1 through 12.

2. On the bottom of each saucer, write an addition or subtraction problem that will equal the numerals 1 through 12. (You should have only one answer for each problem; each teacup has only one saucer to match it.)

3. Working in groups of two or three, ask students to find the correct matches by solving the problem.

4. To go further, use the cups and saucers along with other dishes (such as dessert plates) and utensils (such as spoons) for a pretend tea party. Ask children to set the table for 12, using one-to-one correspondence. To reinforce one-to-one correspondence, label the teacups with a numeral and the saucers with a group of dots that match the numeral.

Arachnophobia!

Where is Miss Spider hiding? Students use critical-thinking skills, number sense, and the process of elimination to find Miss Spider. You will need 12 paper cups (or the teacups from Time for Tea) and a small plastic spider to set up the activity.

1. Turn the cups upside down and write the numerals 1 through 12 on the cups where they can be clearly seen.

2. Hide a small plastic spider under one of the cups.

3. In order to determine which cup Miss Spider is under, have children ask questions about the cups' numerals and positions—for example, "Is Miss Spider hiding in a cup that is between the numerals 4 and 7?" Encourage children to use positional (*next to, between*) and number words (*two, three*) in their questions.

4. When a child guesses the hiding place of Miss Spider, he or she takes a turn hiding the spider. The rest of the class asks questions, trying to locate Miss Spider.

Tip

To extend the Time for Tea activity, host your own Miss Spider's Tea Party! Make the party very fancy, using real sugar cubes and caffeine-free tea. Serve pastries, and remind students to use their fancy manners. Include more math skills by having students use one-to-one correspondence as they set the table.

Book Links

Counting comes alive with these books:

Counting Crocodiles
by Judy Sierra
(Gulliver Books, 1997)

A hungry monkey spies a banana on an island but must cross a sea of crocodiles to get to the banana. The monkey succeeds as he counts the crocodiles one through ten and back again.

How Many Bugs in a Box?
by David Carter
(Little Simon, 1988)

This lift-the-flap counting book uses fanciful descriptions for each bug, while counting them from one to ten.

The Icky Bug Counting Book
by Jerry Pallotta
(Charlesbridge, 1992)

This book not only teaches counting but is also filled with facts about insects as an added bonus.

1 Is One
by Tasha Tudor
(Simon and Schuster, 2000)

Adapted from the original 1956 Caldecott Honor book, this book counts from one to 20 not only with numerals but also with number words.

We're Going Buggy!

Put bugs to work to teach the concept of place value and the base-ten number system.

1. Make base-ten sticks by gluing small plastic bugs to craft sticks (ten each). Make enough sticks for each child in your class to have two or three.

2. Give each student two or three base-ten bug sticks, ten individual bugs, and a paper plate to represent Miss Spider's table.

3. Make up bug number stories to tell students, or reread portions of *Miss Spider's Tea Party*. Ask children to place the number of bugs that you say aloud in the story on their paper plates. For example, you may say, "Two bugs came to Miss Spider's for tea, and soon after, five more bugs joined them." (Students would place two and then five bugs on their plates.)

4. Whenever students find they have ten bugs on the plate, have them call out "Ten's too many!" At this point, have them reorganize the bugs on their plates, using base-ten sticks plus individual bugs to make the number requested.

Make 12

Miss Spider counts to 12 in the book *Miss Spider's Tea Party*. Give students a chance to work with 12 items with this center activity.

1. Gather many different manipulatives, such as stacking cubes, base-ten blocks, coins, base-ten bug sticks (We're Going Buggy!, above), individual plastic bugs, and any others you wish to use.

2. Ask students to use the manipulatives to make the number 12 as many ways as they can. You will see many displays, such as a dime and two pennies, a stack of ten cubes and two left separately, and 12 items all grouped together.

3. Ask students to explain their approach to the problem, using questioning techniques that reveal their thinking and reasoning.

Hannah's Collections

by Marthe Jocelyn

◆ ◆

(DUTTON CHILDREN'S BOOKS, 2000)

When Hannah's teacher asks that each child bring in a collection of things, Hannah faces a dilemma, because she has collections of so many things: leaves, buttons, shells, feathers, and many other objects, all of which she loves to sort, classify, and count! She can't decide which collection to bring. Finally, Hannah makes a sculpture of all her collections and begins to collect . . . sculptures, of course!

Before Reading

Children love to sort and classify things. Just give a child a button box on a rainy day, and watch how many combinations they get sorted into. It's the teacher's job to take this informal mathematical knowledge and provide a bridge to the more formal mathematics we use in school. Invite students to share collections they have, and ways they have sorted their collections. As you read the book aloud, invite them to notice if they've sorted their collections in any of the same ways Hannah organizes her collections.

After Reading

Sorting and classifying items helps children learn to make generalizations about things, which helps them to better connect knowledge from one situation to another. For example, when a child sorts buttons, that knowledge is transferred to other sorting situations, such as identifying numbers as even and odd. Get students thinking about different ways to sort and classify with these prompts.

◎ At the end of the book, Hannah decided to make a sculpture with all her collections. What do you think about this idea?

◎ Does the sculpture easily show the different collections? Explain.

◎ How would you organize the collections so they would be more easily visible? (Encourage students to think creatively about different ways to display the collections, providing examples of ways to sort when necessary.)

Meeting the Math Standards

Number and Operations

◆ Understanding numbers and representing them in different ways

◆ Connecting numerals and number words to their quantities

Algebra

◆ Sorting and classifying

Tip

▲▲▲▲▲▲

Promote mathematical reasoning by inviting children to share their own collections and explain how they've sorted them. In advance, you might invite students in the audience to try to identify the organizational structure of each collection. For example, they might notice that a classmate's rock collection is sorted into two groups: sparkly, not sparkly.

Scavenger Hunt

Strengthen sorting and classifying skills with a nature scavenger hunt.

1. Give each child a "collection" bag. Explain to children that they will be collecting things on their nature scavenger hunt. Before heading off on the hunt, outline the types of things students can collect—for example, leaves, pebbles, and pinecones, but no living things. (To make the sorting part of this activity more manageable, you might limit the number of items children place in their bags.)

2. When you return from the hunt, set out several large trays (lunch trays or clean polystyrene trays), and label them according to what students collected—"Leaves," "Pebbles," and so on.

3. Invite children to take turns sharing the contents of their bag, placing each item on the appropriate tray in the process.

4. When all students have shared their collections, place the trays in the science center and encourage students to explore new ways to sort the objects. For example, they might further sort leaves by shape or pinecones by size. (Provide additional trays for this purpose.)

Sort-by-Number Muffin Game

Representing numbers in different ways helps children become more mathematically literate. This sorting game incorporates using numbers in different ways to accomplish this goal.

1. Gather the following materials: bingo chips (24), paper muffin cups (six), a six-muffin baking tin, and a die.

2. Label the bingo chips with four different variations each of the numbers one through six. For example, show the number three on four different chips as the numeral (3), the word (three), with tally marks (|||), and with pips arranged as on a die (⦂).

3. On the inside bottom of the muffin cups, write the numerals 1 through 6. Place the muffin cups in the muffin tin.

4. Mix up the chips and place them faceup in the middle of two to four players.

5. Each player takes a turn rolling a die and choosing any bingo chip that matches the number rolled. The player places the bingo chip in the matching muffin cup.

6. Players continue taking turns in this way until all the chips are in a muffin cup.

Tip

▲▲▲▲▲▲

When children become practiced at playing the game with the numbers one through six, add another die, and a muffin tin and bingo chips for the numbers seven through 12. For a variation, give each player his or her own muffin tin and muffin cups. When the game is over, invite students to compare the number of chips they have for each number.

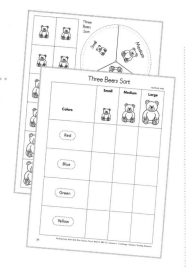

Three Bears Sort

Children will be learning without even realizing it when they play this game of sorting by size and color.

1. Photocopy the following materials: Three Bears Sorting Mat (page 24; one for each player), teddy bear counters (page 25; one set for each player), "Color" and "Size" spinners (page 25; one set for each group of two to four players).

2. Let children color the teddy bear counters red, blue, green, and yellow (one of each color/size). They might also like to color the sorting mats. Assemble the spinners: Cut out each spinner and glue it to a sheet of tagboard for durability. Color the "Color" spinner sections as indicated (red, blue, green, and yellow). Attach an arrow to the center of each spinner with a brass fastener.

3. Guide children in following these steps to play:

   • Place the teddy bear counters in the center of the playing area.

   • Each player takes a turn spinning both spinners. The player takes a bear counter that matches both spinner attributes (color and size) and places it on his or her sorting mat. For example, a player who spins a "medium" on the size spinner and a "red" on the color spinner would place a medium red bear on the appropriate box of the sorting mat.

   • The person to fill the game mat first is the winner! For a cooperative version, children can play with one mat and work together to fill it.

Set Puzzlers

Encourage children to use math vocabulary in their conversations, while strengthening critical-thinking skills and sorting.

1. Using collections of small objects, game pieces, or attribute sorting manipulatives, make a set and display it for children to see.

2. Ask children to guess what attribute you sorted by. For example, if all the items are red, children might guess that you sorted by color.

3. Invite the student who correctly guesses the sorting attribute to take a turn creating a new set puzzler for the class to solve.

4. For a variation, create sets with attributes that students represent. Sort them by attributes, such as first names that start with the same letter. Invite the students with the shared attribute to stand.

Book Links

Reinforce concepts of sorting and classifying with these read-alouds:

Goldilocks and the Three Bears
retold by James Marshall (Dial Books, 1988)

This Caldecott Honor book tells the classic story of Goldilocks in the three bears' house. Look for all the ways Goldilocks sorts the bears' household items.

Grandma's Button Box
by Linda Williams Aber (Kane Press, 2002)

When Grandma's button box falls, scattering buttons all over the floor, Kelly and her cousins sort the buttons by several different attributes.

Harriet's Halloween Candy
by Nancy Carlson (Carolrhoda Books, 1982)

Harriet sorts Halloween candy by size, color, and favorites, and finally shares some with her little brother.

Tip

Teddy bear counters in different sizes and colors are available from Lakeshore Learning Materials (lakeshorelearning.com; 800-778-4456).

Three Bears Sort

Colors	Small	Medium	Large
Red			
Blue			
Green			
Yellow			

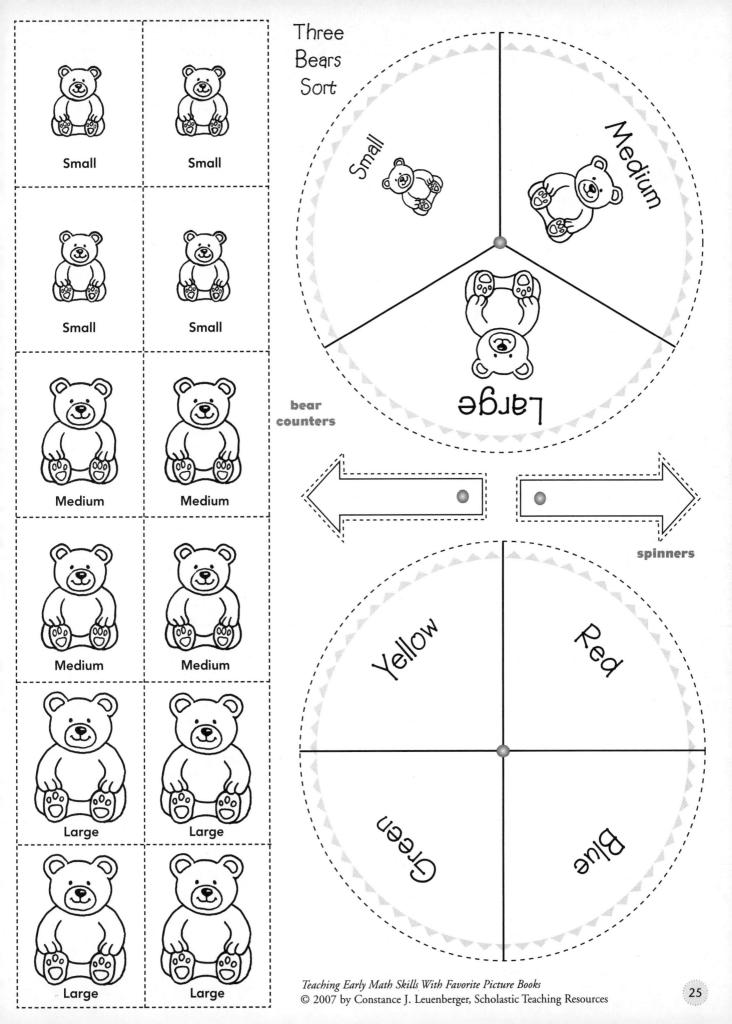

Three
Bears
Sort

Small

Medium

Large

bear
counters

spinners

Small | Small

Small | Small

Medium | Medium

Medium | Medium

Large | Large

Large | Large

Yellow

Red

Green

Blue

Teaching Early Math Skills With Favorite Picture Books
© 2007 by Constance J. Leuenberger, Scholastic Teaching Resources

Thump, Thump, Rat-a-Tat-Tat

by Gene Baer

(HARPERCOLLINS, 1989)

Meeting the Math Standards

Algebra

◆ Recognizing, describing, and extending patterns in sounds and sequences

This pattern book has a marching band parading through it with bright, bold color, and the repeating sound pattern "THUMP, THUMP, Rat-a-tat-tat." The parade begins in the distance and as it arrives, readers see "Festive colors Flashing brass" proceeding onward into the horizon.

Before Reading

Children love music, and they'll enjoy finding the musical pattern in this vibrant book. Before reading the book aloud, invite students to share what they know about patterns. Remind students that all patterns do not have to be visual; some patterns can be heard, such as those in music. Then invite students to listen for a pattern as they listen to the story.

After Reading

It's never too early to start pointing out the writer's craft to young learners. Encourage students' natural responses to books by pointing out some of the characteristics in *Thump, Thump, Rat-a-Tat-Tat.* Use these questions to spark a discussion with your students:

◎ Why do you think the words in this book are of different sizes?

◎ What clues tell you the parade is coming, and later passing by?

◎ What kinds of words does the author use to make us feel like we are actually at a parade?

Musical Patterns

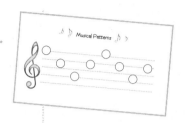

Hearing patterns gives children another way to understand them. Take that a step further by inviting your students to actually "play" some patterns.

1. Gather the following materials: small stickers in different colors (such as the round ones used to price items at yard sales), various musical instruments, and several copies of the musical patterns template (page 29; enlarge the template if desired).

2. Use small stickers to label each type of musical instrument by color. For example, all drums may have a blue sticker, horns a red sticker, and xylophones a green sticker.

3. Color in the circles on the reproducible musical patterns to match the stickers on the instruments and make a musical pattern. For example, make an A-B pattern by coloring the circles in an alternating red-blue order (to indicate horn, drum, horn, drum, and so on). Create several patterns, incorporating the use of different instruments and different patterns. Tape several strips together to create a longer pattern.

4. Invite children to "play" the patterns, using the colored circles to tell which instrument to play, and when. When children are adept at following the musical patterns, they can create their own musical patterns to play.

Marching Band Patterns

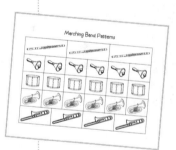

Research tells us that children's learning experiences with patterns help them to better understand numbers, counting, and problem solving. (McClain, K. & P. Cobb, 1999) Increase their understanding with this hands-on learning activity.

1. Give each child a sentence strip and a copy of the marching band patterns (page 29). Invite children to color the instruments on the pattern page and cut them out.

2. Have children arrange the instruments on the sentence strip to make a pattern. When they are satisfied with the placement, they can glue the instruments in place.

3. Use an O-ring to bind the sentence strips together to make a class pattern book. Bring students together to share the book. Children can identify and describe their instrument patterns—for example, A-B, A-B-C or AA-BB—as you share each page with the class. Consider "playing" each pattern by using different sounds for each instrument picture—for example, clap hands and snap fingers for an A-B pattern.

Reinforce concepts of patterning with read-alouds that invite children to chime in:

Chicka Chicka Boom Boom
by Bill Martin Jr. and
John Archambault
(Simon and Schuster, 1989)

This rhythmic chanting book repeats the phrase "Chicka Chicka Boom Boom, will there be enough room?" as each letter of the alphabet tries to climb the coconut tree.

Chicken Soup With Rice
by Maurice Sendak
(HarperCollins, 1962)

Kids love to sing along with this song of months, repeating the catchy "chicken soup with rice" pattern at the end of each verse.

The Napping House
by Audrey Wood
(Harcourt, 1984)

Children will delight in the cumulative, repetitive text and clever pictures depicting a houseful of sleepers in this classic book.

Why Mosquitoes Buzz in People's Ears
by Verna Aardema
(Dial, 1975)

Using onomatopoeia and a cumulative patterning format, this African tale (a Caldecott medal winner) explains the chain of events that occurs when a mosquito says something foolish to an iguana.

Choral Reading Patterns

Choral reading not only solidifies reading concepts with young students but helps them feel the repetition of patterning as well.

1. If possible, obtain a big book copy of *Thump, Thump, Rat-a-Tat-Tat*. If a big book version is unavailable, write the words "Thump, Thump, Thump, Thump," and "Rat-a-tat-tat" on chart paper for easy reading.

2. Divide the class into two groups. Explain that as you reread *Thump, Thump, Rat-a-Tat-Tat*, one group will join in on the words "THUMP, THUMP," while the other group will chime in on "Rat-a-tat-tat." Encourage students to notice the sound patterns they make as they read along.

3. After reading, invite students to point out patterns they heard (A-B, A-B-B-A, and so on).

Patterns All Around

To further reinforce for students the concept of patterning, look no further than your school!

1. Use a digital camera to take photos of things that you find around the school (or around town) that occur in patterns— for example, a striped pattern on curtains or a brick pattern on a wall. If you wish, take close-ups of the patterns to disguise the subject matter.

2. Bind the photos into a class book. Bring students together to share the photos. How many places can they identify by looking at the patterns? Take a walk around school, with the book in hand, to locate patterns in the photos. What is surprising to students as they look at the photos and the actual subject matter?

3. Encourage students to visit the book again and again on their own. What new discoveries can they make in the patterns they see? What other patterns can they find in their school to add to the book?

Musical Patterns

Marching Band Patterns

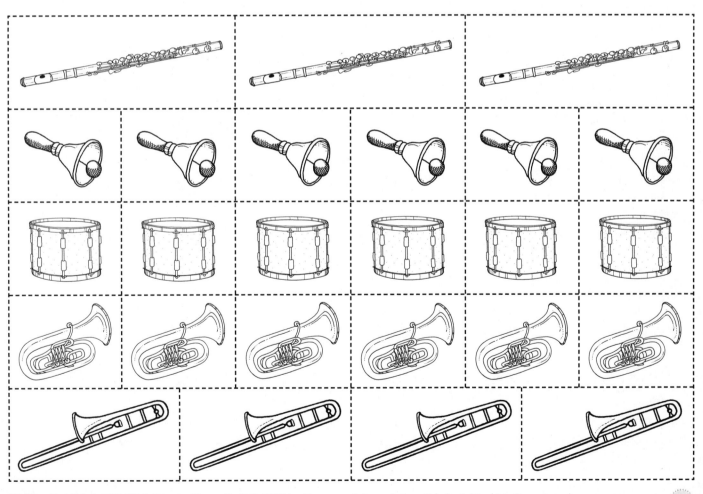

12 Ways to Get to 11

by Eve Merriam

◆

(SIMON AND SCHUSTER, 1993)

Meeting the Math Standards

Number and Operations

◆ Using computation and building fluency in addition and subtraction

◆ Using mental computation, as well as using manipulatives to compute

Algebra

◆ Showing the commutative property of numbers

◆ Using pictures and verbal representations to show number sentences

Where is 11? Is it at the circus with "six peanut shells and five pieces of popcorn"? Or is it in the mailbox with "seven letters, two packages, a mail-order catalog, and a picture postcard"? In 12 clever ways, the author explores different number combinations that equal 11.

Before Reading

Read the title of the book, and ask: "Why do you think the author chose this title?" Invite students to share ideas, and then have them continue to think about this as they listen to the story. Encourage children to think about the different ways the author writes about "getting to 11," and to carefully follow each two-page spread to better understand what combinations of numbers equal 11.

After Reading

Use these questions to further explore the author's title choice and the different ways she gets to 11.

◎ Now why do you think the author called this book *12 Ways to Get to 11*?

◎ Which was your favorite way to get to 11?

◎ (Revisit the spreads in the book and have children count them.) What is the twelfth way to get to 11?

◎ (Look at the last two pages with the chicks taking off across the spread.) If you were the author, what would you write to go with the picture on these pages?

Making 11

Use this book as another opportunity for children to demonstrate commutativity of numbers using concrete examples.

1. Give each child 11 interlocking cubes.

2. Reread the book, inviting students to show the different ways to make 11 on each page. For example, for "Out of the magician's hat: four banners, five rabbits, a pitcher of water, and a bouquet of flowers," students would show a stack of four cubes, five cubes, one cube (standing alone), and another cube (standing alone). Then have students combine their cubes saying "plus" as they add each group together to make 11 (for example, "Four plus five plus one plus one equals 11").

3. On chart paper, record each new way students make 11.

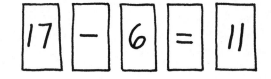

Tip

To reinforce making number sentences with the problems from the book, place the book at a center along with counters of some type (for example, interlocking cubes, trading chips, or wooden cubes). Invite students to use the counters and problems in the book to make number sentences with manipulatives and record them on paper.

Math on the Move

In this whole-group activity, students manipulate numbers and symbols (+, –, =) as they experiment with different ways to make number sentences, part of the patterning found in math.

1. On index cards, write the numerals 0 through 20 (make two cards for 11), an addition sign, a subtraction sign, and an equal sign (one numeral or symbol per card).

2. Give each child a card. (Depending on the number of students, some may have more than one card or you may need to use additional numbers to create more cards.)

3. Invite children who have the equal sign card and one of the number 11 cards to stand in front of the class in that order (= 11).

4. Call out a number. The child with that card joins the children in front, standing to the right of the child with the = card. These children then decide which numeral and mathematical sign (addition or subtraction) they need to make a true number sentence. For example, if 17 was called, the children with the 17, =, and 11 cards might decide they need to subtract and will call children with the 6 and – cards to join them. These children then organize themselves to create the number sentence 17 – 6 = 11.

5. Repeat with new numbers until everyone has at least one chance to form a true number sentence.

Book Links

These books give your students more opportunities to explore the commutative property of numbers:

Domino Addition
by Lynette Long
(Charlesbridge, 1996)

Using illustrations of dominoes, this book encourages children to learn addition facts to 12.

Mission Addition
by Loreen Leedy
(Holiday House, 1997)

In this colorful book, Miss Prime and her enthusiastic students make up word problems, create addition sentences, and check their work.

One Hundred Hungry Ants
by Elinor J. Pinczes
(Houghton Mifflin, 1993)

One hundred hungry ants march off to a picnic, reorganizing themselves in different number combinations to get there more quickly.

Two Ways to Count to Ten: A Liberian Folktale
by Ruby Dee
(Henry Holt, 1988)

King Leopard must decide who will marry his daughter and become the new ruler, so he develops a test: Whoever can throw a spear in the air for the count of ten will win. One by one the animals fail, until the antelope comes up with some clever counting.

Nine Ways to Get to Eight Mini-Book

Encourage students to use what they learn about the commutative property of numbers to create a mini-book with new number sentences and number families.

1. Give each child ten sheets of paper (half sheets are fine).

2. Have children copy the book title on the cover page and write their name. On the remaining pages, have children draw pictures and write a number sentence to show how they get to eight. For example, a child might draw a picture of four bananas and four oranges to equal eight in all, and then write the number sentence $4 + 4 = 8$. Another child might draw one sun, four flowers, and three bees, and write $1 + 4 + 3 = 8$. To go further, children can include words that tell what makes eight on each page.

Five Golden Rings

To explore the commutative property of numbers, invite students to make sums of five with this sparkling activity.

1. Use five inexpensive play rings to model this activity. Place some rings on one hand and remaining rings on the other. Trace your hands on paper and draw the rings as placed on your hands. Write a number sentence to match the ring distribution—for example, $1 + 4 = 5$.

2. Invite children to make sums of five by placing rings on the fingers of each hand. For example, two rings on one hand and three rings on the other will make five.

3. To create a record, have children trace their hands on paper and draw the rings they placed on each finger. Have students write a number sentence to match their drawing.

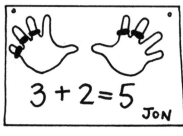

3 + 2 = 5   JON

Emily's First 100 Days of School

by Rosemary Wells

◆

(HYPERION, 2000)

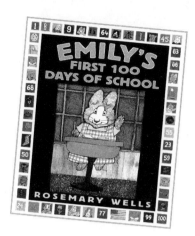

"On the first day of school I leave my mama's arms. I am too excited to cry." And so it goes in this endearing book of the first 100 days of school. As the story continues, Emily discovers how she has changed and grown: learning to read and write and making new friends. Before long, the one-hundredth day of school arrives!

Before Reading

One hundred days can seem like an eternity in the life of a young child. The NCTM standards outline the importance of qualitative (a child growing taller) and quantitative change (a child growing three inches in one year). Discuss these kinds of changes with students. Ask children how much they think they can grow in 100 days. Invite students to estimate how much they think they can learn in 100 days. Accept all answers. Then encourage children to find the ways Emily changed over the course of 100 days of school.

After Reading

In order for children to make sense of their world, it is important for them to understand that change happens over time, and that it is sometimes predictable (such as children growing) and sometimes not predictable. Invite students to make connections to the changes in the book as they consider change in their lives and surroundings. Use the following questions to elicit responses:

◎ In what ways have you changed since the beginning of the school year?

◎ Are you older or younger? Do people always grow older, or do they grow younger?

◎ Do you think growing older is a predictable change (something that you can count on happening)?

◎ Have you grown taller since last year? Do children usually grow taller in a year's time?

◎ What are some ways to record these kinds of changes?

Meeting the Math Standards

Number and Operations

◆ Counting

Algebra

◆ Analyzing change, especially qualitative and quantitative change

Student Scrapbooks

Children will delight in their accomplishments in an activity that helps them analyze change over time. Parents will also love the resulting keepsake scrapbooks.

1. At the beginning of every month, give each child a large sheet of drawing paper. At the top of the paper, have children write their name, the month, and the year.

2. Have children choose a work sample from the month and glue it on the page. Children can then add other records from the month, such as their height, a picture showing a way they've changed (or a photo), and a brief, positive teacher report. Place each month's pages in a folder for children.

3. On the one-hundredth day of school, pull out the book pages and have students arrange them in order. Have them notice ways in which they've grown. If possible, measure quantitative change of each child's height. This might be just a little bit or sometimes more.

4. Continue creating scrapbook pages until the end of the school year, when children can make covers, place all pages in order, and staple to bind, and then take them home as keepsakes of their year.

Number Journals

Children begin to understand number concepts and qualitative and quantitative change while keeping a collaborative number journal.

1. Make a class number journal by placing 100 sheets of paper in a three-ring binder. (Or use a 100-page spiral bound sketch pad.) Add a cover, either inserting it into a sleeve on the binder cover or gluing it to the front of the sketch pad.

2. As in the book *Emily's First 100 Days of School*, each day invite a volunteer to write the numeral (and number word if desired) in the book that corresponds to the number of days of school.

3. Use shared or interactive writing to add a sentence to the page about the number, as Emily did in her journal. Encourage children to be creative with the numbers, and think of times they have used the number in their lives. For example, on the twelfth day of school a child may write "There are 12 panes on our classroom window. Twelve is a dozen!" On the twenty-third day of school, children might write "There are 23 children in our class!" Let children draw pictures on the page to illustrate the sentence. Continue for 100 days of school to create your own "First 100 Days of School" book!

Tip

As a variation on the collaborative number journals, children can keep individual journals.

Temperature Change

Make math meaningful and relate it to everyday activities by measuring change over 100 days of school.

1. Place an outdoor thermometer in an area that is safe and accessible to children. Each day, check the temperature with students and record it on a calendar.

2. On the one-hundredth day of school, ask children to compare the temperature with the temperature on the first day of school. To measure the temperature qualitatively, ask children if it is warmer or colder on the one-hundredth day than it was on the first day. To compare the temperatures quantitatively, measure the difference in temperature between the two days. Be sure to use the math language "quantitative" and "qualitative" and explain the meaning of each to children.

Class Time Lines

Emily created a time line in the book *Emily's First 100 Days of School* as she documented something that happened each day. Support your students in recognizing change by keeping a class time line.

1. On a roll of adding machine tape, write numerals to correspond to the number of days of school (such as 1–182). Display the tape near the calendar area of your classroom.

2. Throughout the year, take photos of special projects and children in action, and place these photos above the day on which they were taken. For example, if the class visited a senior citizens center on day 42 of the school year, take a photo and place it above the numeral 42 on the adding machine tape.

3. Take time to discuss with children qualitative changes they see in their time line throughout the school year.

Book Links

These books about the one-hundredth day of school reinforce the concept of qualitative and quantitative change, as well as counting to 100:

Miss Bindergarten Celebrates the 100th Day of Kindergarten
by Joseph Slate
(Dutton Children's Books, 1998)

Miss Bindergarten requests that in honor of the one-hundredth day of school, each child must bring in "100 of some wonderful, one-hundred-full thing!"

100 Days of School
by Trudy Harris
(Millbrook Press, 1999)

Rhyming text and brilliant illustrations explain how to count to 100 by ones, fives, tens, and twenties.

The 100th Day of School
by Angela Shelf Medearis
(Cartwheel Books, 1996)

A class counts to the one-hundredth day of school and celebrates by learning 100 spelling words, planting 100 seeds, and many other activities.

100th Day Worries
by Margery Cuyler
(Simon and Schuster, 2000)

When Jessica's teacher announces on the ninety-fifth day of school that each student is expected to bring in a collection of 100 things on the one-hundredth day of school, Jessica gets worried.

Color Zoo

by Lois Ehlert

❖

(HARPERCOLLINS, 1989)

Meeting the Math Standards

Number and Operations

◆ Counting and recognizing numbers in a set

Geometry

◆ Recognizing characteristics of two-dimensional shapes

◆ Naming, drawing, building, and comparing two-dimensional shapes

◆ Describing attributes of shapes

◆ Investigating creating two-dimensional shapes

◆ Making mental images of geometric shapes, using visualization and memory

◆ Representing shapes from different perspectives

This 1990 Caldecott Honor book uses enough colors and shapes to fill a zoo! Each page has a cutout shape that, when stacked with the pages beneath it, forms an animal. Three series of shapes are used to form the animals: circles, squares, and triangles; rectangles, ovals, and hearts; and diamonds, octagons, and hexagons. Each shape and animal is boldly labeled in this vibrant picture book.

Before Reading

This book's unusual format actively engages children in exploring shapes as they look to see what picture is forming with each turn of the page. Before reading, invite children to share what they know about shapes, using shapes around the classroom as examples. Reinforce that a shape is still the same shape, whether it is turned upside down, on its side, or sitting upright. As you read, point out shapes that have been turned at different angles, and remind children that they are still called their shape name. (A triangle is still a triangle whether turned upside down or right side up.)

After Reading

"Heads and ears, beaks and snouts,
That's what animals are all about."

To reinforce the way illustrations and text work together, revisit pages in the book, and use the following questions to guide observations. On chart paper, make a list of all the shapes children find in the book and draw pictures (showing different orientations) of each. Ask:

◎ What shape do you think the author would use for heads? Where do you see that shape?

◎ What other shapes do you see here? What part of an animal does that shape remind you of?

◎ What kind of animal has a beak? What shape do you see in a beak?

◎ What part of an animal is its snout? What shapes do you see in a snout?

Animal Shape Books

Invite students to explore shapes as they build their own shape pictures and create a class book.

1. To prepare, cut out several shapes of different colors and sizes. Include the shapes from *Color Zoo* and add others as desired. Your shape set might include the following shapes: circle, square, triangle, rectangle, oval, heart, rhombus, octagon, hexagon, trapezoid, and parallelogram.

2. Place the shapes, colorful construction paper, markers, and glue at a center.

3. Invite children to make their own animal shapes by gluing the shapes to construction paper. Encourage them to experiment with their shape arrangements before gluing, so they can easily make adjustments.

4. Assist children as needed in writing the names of the animals and labeling the shapes they used. Then bind the pages to make a class book. To encourage use of mathematical language in students' conversations, invite them to share their pages, identifying and explaining the shapes they used.

Follow the Directions

Students explore the characteristics of two-dimensional shapes and positions in space as they try their hand at making shapes.

1. You will need a small magic board (whiteboard), or chalkboard with chalk, for yourself and each child. (Children can do this activity in small groups if you do not have a class set of materials.)

2. Without showing students what you are drawing, draw a shape on your magic board and briefly reveal it to them. Invite students to draw the same shape on their board.

3. As children become proficient at this task, try giving verbal directions for students to follow (rather than showing them the shape)—for example, "I would like you to draw a shape with three sides."

4. As a variation, and to reinforce spatial visualization, provide directions that include multiple shapes and positions on the board—for example, "Draw a square in the middle of your board. Now draw a circle under the square and a triangle inside the circle."

Tip

Pattern block task cards can be ordered from any school supply catalog. You can also create your own by making pictures with pattern blocks and then tracing the pattern blocks.

Book Links

These books will engage students in exploring geometric shapes from many perspectives:

Color Farm
by Lois Ehlert
(Lippincott, 1990)

This barnyard version of Ehlert's book *Color Zoo* introduces young readers to farm animals made from different shapes.

Grandfather Tang's Story: A Tale Told With Tangrams
by Ann Tompert
(Crown, 1990)
Grandfather Tang and Little Soo use their tangram shapes to tell magical stories.

The Secret Birthday Message
by Eric Carle
(HarperTrophy, 1986)

A young boy follows a secret map made with shapes to find a birthday gift.

Spinning for Patterns

In this game for two players, children take turns using shapes to build pictures. You'll need a set of pattern blocks, a die, and pattern block task cards. (See Tip, left.)

1. Players place a pile of pattern blocks in the center of the playing area. Each player selects a pattern block task card.

2. The first player rolls the die, takes that number of pattern blocks (in any shape), and places the blocks on the task card in the corresponding places. The second player takes a turn in the same way.

3. Play continues in this way until one player fills the task card. For a cooperative version, children can work together to fill one card.

Can You Make What I Make?

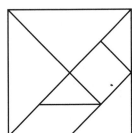

A tangram is an ancient seven-piece Chinese puzzle. This tangram game for two players reinforces spatial memory and visualization.

1. Enlarge and copy the tangram patterns (below), and give each child a set. Students can color the patterns as they wish.

2. Have students pair up to play. PLAYER 1 secretly builds a shape picture using some (but not all) of the seven pieces. (PLAYER 2 can face away.)

3. PLAYER 1 briefly reveals the picture to the other player, and then covers it. PLAYER 2 attempts to build the same picture from memory.

4. PLAYER 1 then reveals the picture once more, and PLAYER 2 makes any necessary corrections while looking at the picture. Players then trade places and repeat.

Tangram Patterns

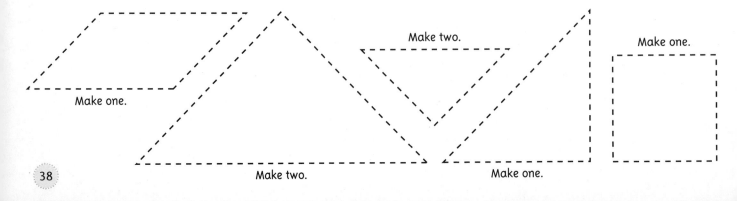

Make one.

Make two.

Make two.

Make one.

Make one.

Eight Hands Round: A Patchwork Alphabet

by Ann Whitford Paul

❖

(HARPERCOLLINS, 1991)

Contemplating the origins of 26 quilt patterns, one for each letter of the alphabet, the author introduces the beautiful geometric designs of quilting. Each pattern is shown as a single section, and as the entire quilt. A story accompanies each quilt, explaining its importance in early American life.

Before Reading

Math Talk
"+ – ÷ × "

Quilts are known for geometric patterns that use slides, flips, turns, and symmetry. If possible, bring in a quilt to share with students. Invite them to point out the shapes they see. Remind them to closely observe the quilt pictures and look for shapes as you read the book aloud. Ask them to notice if some shapes are used more often than others. Point out that each individual quilt square looks far less complicated than the whole quilt.

After Reading

Book Talk
" "

Quilts are a beautiful example of symmetry and geometry. After reading the book *Eight Hands Round: A Patchwork Alphabet*, revisit the quilts in the book. Encourage discussion from children by asking these questions:

◎ What shapes do you recognize in the quilts? (On chart paper, make a list of all the shapes students find.)

◎ Where do you see symmetry in the quilts? (Explain symmetry if needed.)

◎ Why do you think people give quilts special names? Do the shapes in the quilts have something to do with their name?

Meeting the Math Standards

Geometry

◆ Applying transformations with geometric shapes

◆ Recognizing symmetry

◆ Recognizing and using slides, flips, and turns in geometry

Crazy Quilt

Quilts are a part of American heritage and have been around for centuries. Invite children to explore the beauty and geometry of quilts with this activity.

1. In advance, pick up some quilting magazines such as *The Quilter*, *Quilting*, or *Country Quilting*. Check a library, local craft or fabric stores, or bookstores. Thrift shops sometimes carry back issues.

2. Invite students to peruse the magazines, finding one or two quilts they especially like. They can write their names on sticky notes and use these to mark the pages.

3. Give each child a 6- by 6-inch sheet of paper. Have students draw a quilt square based on one of their favorite quilts.

4. Place a large sheet of mural paper (tape paper together if necessary) in an open area. Have children work together to arrange their quilt squares on the paper to make a class "crazy quilt." When students are satisfied with their arrangement, they can glue their squares in place.

5. Display the crazy quilt, and let students take turns discussing the squares they contributed, naming shapes in it, pointing out examples of symmetry, and so on.

Quilting Bee Book

Turn your classroom into a quilting bee as children use geometric flips and turns, as well as symmetry, to create pattern block quilt squares for a collaborative book.

1. Give each child two 6- by 6-inch sheets of paper and assorted pattern block shapes cut from construction paper. Children will also need pattern blocks.

2. Invite children to arrange pattern blocks on one of the squares of paper to create a quilt pattern. When they are satisfied with their pattern, have children glue the construction paper pattern block shapes to the remaining square of paper to re-create their pattern.

3. Have children glue their quilt pattern square on a larger sheet of paper, and then write the name of their pattern and explain why they chose this name.

Flannel Board Tangrams

This activity engages children in using geometric slides, flips, and turns, as well as visualization skills.

1. Gather the following materials: a class set of the tangram pattern (enlarge the patterns on page 38), a set of felt tangram shapes, and a felt board.

2. Give each child a tangram pattern. Invite children to color or decorate the shapes.

3. Use two or three felt tangram pieces to create a shape on the flannel board.

4. Briefly show the shape to students, and then have them re-create the shape from memory with their tangram.

5. Reveal your shape to students, and allow them to make adjustments to their shapes as necessary to make them match.

6. Continue, making the shapes increasingly more involved, with more pieces, as children become more adept at visualizing the shapes and re-creating them.

7. As a follow-up, set up a center area with the book *Eight Hands Round: A Patchwork Alphabet*, a flannel board, and the flannel tangram, and invite children to experiment with different geometric shapes.

Geoboard Reflections

Children work with geometric slides, flips, and turns to create mirror images.

1. Give each pair of children two geoboards and rubber bands. You will also need a mirror.

2. Have one child in each pair use the rubber bands to create a pattern on the geoboard (try simple patterns at first), and then hold up the geoboard to a mirror.

3. Observing the geoboard in the mirror, the second child re-creates the design from the mirror's perspective.

4. Children compare their boards and check to see if the second is a mirror image.

Tip

▲▲▲▲▲▲

Reinforce geometric concepts with the NCTM Illuminations Patch Tool activity (illuminations.nctm.org/ Activities.aspx?grade=1). Students can use this online activity to create quilt patterns, applying slides, flips, and turns in the process.

Book Links

••••••••• ◆ •••••••••

These books invite readers to explore shapes in different ways, including by noticing them in the environment and in art:

I Spy Shapes in Art
by Lucy Micklethwait
(Greenwillow, 2004)

Readers are encouraged to find shapes in reproductions of famous paintings.

Mouse Shapes
by Ellen Stoll Walsh
(Harcourt, 2007)

Three sneaky mice manipulate shapes to trick a cat.

Museum Shapes
by the New York Metropolitan Museum of Art
(Little, Brown, 2005)

Incorporating art and math appreciation, this book invites readers to find ten different shapes.

The Shape of Things

by Dayle Ann Dodds

❖❖

(CANDLEWICK PRESS, 1996)

Meeting the Math Standards

Geometry

◆ Understanding characteristics of two- and three-dimensional geometric shapes

◆ Describing attributes and parts of two- and three-dimensional shapes

◆ Composing and decomposing two-dimensional shapes

❝A square is just a square, until you add a roof, two windows and a door, then it's much, much more!" This rhyme introduces readers to a colorful book of shapes. As the book continues, a circle becomes a Ferris wheel, a triangle turns into a boat, and a rectangle is transformed into a train.

Before Reading

For geometrical understandings, children need to be able to name and draw shapes. Encourage these skills with a discussion about the cover illustration. Ask: "What shapes did the illustrator use to create this picture?" (for example, circle, square, rectangle) Invite children to take turns drawing these shapes on chart paper, and then label them. As you share the book, encourage children to focus on these and other shapes used to create each illustration.

After Reading

The geometric shapes in this book are easy to identify, and are good examples of what shapes look like when they are flipped and turned. Revisit pages in the book and use these questions to initiate a discussion about the shapes that make up everyday objects:

◎ What shapes do you see in this picture? Where are some other places we see these shapes?

◎ Do you think using shapes made it easier to create this picture? Why? Using these same shapes, what is something you could draw a picture of?

More Shapes of Things

Using the book *The Shape of Things* as a model, make a class big book about shapes.

1. Cut out construction paper shapes to match those in the book.

2. Invite students to decide what shape they want to use on the first page and what object they want to represent with that shape. For example, the book might begin with a square to represent a gift box. Glue that shape on a large sheet of paper and write the text—for example, "A square is just a square, until you add a ribbon and a bow!"

3. Continue in this way to create as many pages as desired for the book. Then have children enhance the illustrations on each page with crayons, markers, and collage materials.

4. When the book is complete, read it with children. Then display it in the classroom library for children to revisit.

Two-Dimensional and Three-Dimensional Shapes

Comparing shapes helps children recognize attributes of each shape and differentiate between shapes.

1. Make construction paper templates to represent block shapes.

2. Invite children to build block structures.

3. When their structures are complete, have students reproduce them with the construction paper templates.

4. Discuss children's buildings and representations. Ask: "How are the blocks and the templates different? How many sides do different blocks have? Which structure was easier to make: the block structure or the construction paper 'block' version?"

Tip
▲▲▲▲▲▲▲

This activity provides a good opportunity to incorporate interactive writing. As they are able, students can help write the text in the book, based on their developmental writing skills. For example, you might invite some children to fill in a letter that begins their name. Others might write whole words that contain spelling patterns they are learning.

Tip
▲▲▲▲▲▲▲

Students stretch their mathematical thinking when they build tall block structures, and then re-create the structures with construction paper templates on a flat surface. Creating the construction paper representation hones visualization and spatial relations skills.

Book Links

These books introduce readers to shapes in everyday objects, fine art, and more:

Architecture Shapes
by Michael Crosbie and Steve Rosenthal
(Preservation Press, 1993)

Buildings' architectural elements are paired with line drawings of their matching shapes.

Arrow to the Sun: A Pueblo Indian Tale
by Gerald McDermott
(Viking, 1974)

Bold shapes and color characterize this Caldecott-winning adaptation of the ancient Pueblo Indian legend.

Changes, Changes
by Pat Hutchins
(Aladdin, 1987)

In this wordless picture book, wooden people live in a block house until it catches fire, then the blocks transform into a fire engine, and then a boat (to handle all the water) . . .

Shapes
by Philip Yenawine
(The Museum of Modern Art, 2006)

"Can you find buildings? And roofs?" These questions invite young readers to explore shapes in artwork by Picasso, Seurat, Gauguin, and other artists.

Shapes, Shapes, Shapes
by Tana Hoban
(HarperCollins, 1986)

In classic Hoban style, photographs reveal clear shapes of everyday objects.

Potato Prints

Illustrator Julie Lacome is quoted in the back of *The Shape of Things* as saying, "For the borders of each page, I used potato-cut printing, as children do in school—that was the most fun!" Invite students to experiment in a similar way with geometric shapes and potato printing.

1. Slice potatoes in half. Cut different shapes (square, circle, triangle) into the surface of each half. Gather paper and paint (pour into pie tins).

2. Invite students to dip the potatoes in paint and print the shapes on paper.

3. Encourage each child to make several prints (using a separate sheet of paper for each), so they will have enough pages for a book (including a cover).

4. Allow the prints to dry, and then invite children to use markers to turn the shapes into objects such as a house or a flower.

5. Have students label the shapes on each page. Bind children's pages into books they can take home and share with their families.

Environmental Shape Book

Solidify geometry skills by creating an environmental shape book that children can visit again and again!

1. Take photos of common objects with prominent shapes.

2. With a heavy, broad-tipped marker, outline the shape of the object on the photo. For example, if you take a photo of a skyscraper, outline the rectangular shape of the building.

3. Place each photo on a page, and then draw the shape and write its name in the space below the photo.

4. Add the book to your classroom library for endless shape learning and fun!

All You Need for a Snowman

by Alice Schertle

◆❖◆

(H A R C O U R T ,   2 0 0 2)

Rollicking, rhyming language and endearing illustrations make this book about building snowmen a favorite. When the first snowflake begins fluttering down, the bundled children start to make a snowman, using position words to explain the location of each snowball and piece of clothing. The word *except* at the end of most pages urges the reader on.

Meeting the Math Standards

Geometry

◆ Using coordinates to describe spatial relationships

◆ Describing positions in space

◆ Describing direction and distance in space

◆ Using position words, such as *near to, between, on top, below, under,* and *next to*

Before Reading

Math Talk
"+ - × ÷"

Initiate a discussion about snowman building. Ask: "How would you explain how to build a snowman to someone who has never seen snow? What words would you use? What kinds of words would help the snowman builder know exactly how to place the snowballs?" Make a list of the words students generate. As you read the book, invite children to identify words the author uses to describe how to build a snowman and to notice if they used some of the same words.

After Reading

Book Talk
"66 99"

Thinking spatially, by imagining shapes in different positions, is key for mathematical development. After sharing the book, encourage spatial thinking by following up on the position words students suggested:

◎ Did you and the author use any of the same words to describe how to build a snowman? (Identify those words on the list.)

◎ What are some new words the author used? (Add these to the list.)

◎ What are some other ways we can use these words? (Let children experiment with using the position words in new scenarios—for example, they might use some of the words to describe who they sit near: "I sit beside Jordan and in front of Caroline.")

How to Build a Snowman

It's important to help students develop position and spatial sense by using many different position words. Build snowmen any time of the year while you reinforce these important skills!

1. Gather the following materials: play clay, pipe cleaners, buttons, wiggly eyes, and other items children can use to decorate a snowman.

2. Demonstrate the activity by modeling how to build a snowman with the materials. Use position words from the list as you work.

3. Provide pairs of children with a set of materials. One child in each pair begins by using position words to tell the other child how to build a snowman. The other child must build the snowman exactly as his or her partner dictates, even if it doesn't look right.

4. After the first snowman is complete, children trade places and try again. Provide time for children to try this several times, which will allow them to fine-tune their directions and see how this changes the result.

Where's the Snowman?

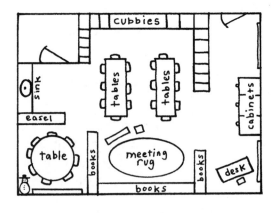

Maps help build children's spatial sense. Send children on a snowman hunt with this map activity.

1. Hide a paper or figurine snowman somewhere in your classroom. Then prepare a map of the classroom that shows how to find the snowman.

2. During class meeting time, explain to students that you have lost a snowman and he is hiding somewhere in the classroom.

3. Show students a map revealing how to locate the snowman. Invite students to help you find him by reading the map.

4. Reinforce map skills by letting children make a map and hide the snowman for their classmates to find.

Snowman Puzzle

Strengthen geometry skills with this coordinate grid snowman puzzle.

1. Give each child a copy of the snowman puzzle (page 48). Copy the grid on chart paper and use it to model how to plot ordered pairs, such as (B, 4).

2. Once students understand the process of plotting ordered pairs, let them take turns coloring in squares on the grid for ordered pairs you name. Explain that with the snowman puzzle pieces, students will plot the ordered pairs in the same way.

3. Have students cut out each snowman piece, arrange the pieces on the grid according to the coordinates, and then glue them in place.

Playground Space

Children benefit from opportunities to experience their body in different spaces, and outdoor play is crucial for child development. Try these fun outdoor activities to reinforce spatial awareness.

1. If you don't have playground equipment, gather some large boxes and other items children can go around, through, over, and so on (such as cones). You can also use chalk to draw on a paved play area.

2. Go outside to the play area and call out directions to students—for example: "Go under the slide. Go around the swing set. Climb through the tunnel [or box]." If you're using boxes, you might say: "Jump over the small box. Climb through the biggest box. Run around the medium box."

3. Students can take turns being the leader and calling out new sets of directions.

Book Links

These books reinforce mapping and spatial relations skills:

Rosie's Walk
by Pat Hutchins
(MacMillan, 1968)

Rosie the hen leaves her chicken coop for a stroll around the barnyard, traveling over, under, and around things, completely oblivious to the sly fox following her.

There's a Map in My Lap!
All About Maps
by Tish Rabe
(Random House, 2002)

In classic silly style, the Cat in the Hat introduces maps of all kinds (city, state, national, topographic).

The Three Billy Goats Gruff
by P. C. Asbjrnsen and J. E. Moe
(Harcourt, 1957)

This classic story of goats trip-trapping over the troll's bridge uses position words, as the billy goats trip-trap over the bridge and the troll maintains his stance under the bridge. This is a great story to act out!

Tip

Don't underestimate the value of outdoor play to develop spatial sense. Be sure young children get outdoor playtime every day. Our vestibular system is responsible for allowing us to maintain balance and move through space. Vestibular stimulation is supported through swinging, climbing, rocking, and jumping—things all young children need time to do.

Build a Snowman

Name _____

Date _____

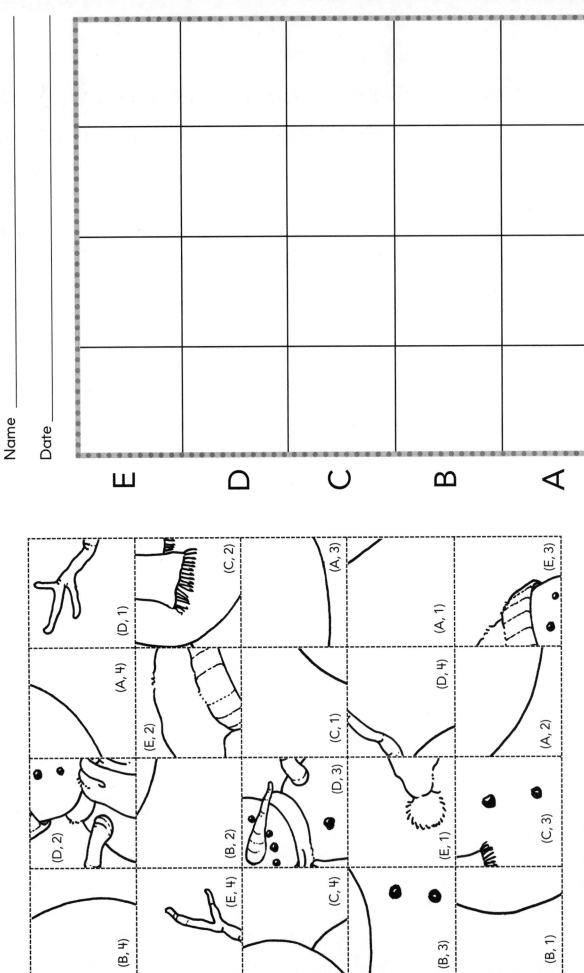

E D C B A

1 2 3 4

(B, 4) | (E, 4) | (C, 4) | (B, 3) | (B, 1)

(D, 2) | (A, 4) | (E, 2) | (B, 2) | (D, 3) | (D, 1) | (C, 2)

(C, 1) | (E, 1) | (C, 3) | (A, 3) | (A, 1) | (D, 4) | (A, 2) | (E, 3)

Teaching Early Math Skills With Favorite Picture Books
© 2007 by Constance J. Leuenberger, Scholastic Teaching Resources

The Littlest Dinosaurs

by Bernard Most

◆

(HARCOURT BRACE JOVANOVICH, 1989)

Comparing dinosaurs to familiar, similar-sized objects provides intriguing measurement experiences for young readers. At the beginning of the book, Most briefly touches on the very largest dinosaurs, and then launches into explanations of the smallest dinosaurs, sequencing them in size order from largest to smallest. Many of these dinosaurs are not much bigger than children, with the last and smallest dinosaur, measuring only eight inches!

Before Reading

Were all dinosaurs huge? Most people think so. Tell children that you will be reading a book to them about the littlest dinosaurs that ever lived. Encourage students to estimate how little they think the smallest dinosaurs were: As big as a car? The size of a dog? As they listen, have children compare the dinosaurs in the book to common objects. Challenge them to figure out the pattern this book follows (largest to smallest).

After Reading

Young children love to compare things, and comparing measurements is an important mathematical skill that gets them ready for more complex measurement understandings. Chart dinosaurs in the book and their sizes. Set up a third column for comparisons. Then guide a discussion that encourages children to make comparisons.

◎ What is surprising to you about the smallest dinosaurs? What are some things in our classroom that are about the same size?

◎ Which dinosaur was closest in size to you? How much bigger or smaller are you?

◎ Which dinosaur was largest? What are some things that are about that size?

Meeting the Math Standards

Measurement

◆ Recognizing and comparing the attributes of length

◆ Measuring length using nonstandard and standard measurement

◆ Selecting appropriate measuring tools for measurement

Book Links

These books highlight basic concepts of measurement:

How Big Were the Dinosaurs?
by Bernard Most
(Harcourt, 1994)

Once again, Most compares dinosaurs to familiar objects, this time focusing on the biggest dinosaurs.

Measuring Penny
by Loreen Leedy
(Holiday House, 1997)

For a measuring homework assignment, Lisa decides to measure her dog, Penny. This book will expand children's thinking about measurement.

Ten Beads Tall
by Pam Adams
(Child's Play, 1990)

This playful book comes with a string of ten beads readers can use to determine the width, height, and length of objects in the pictures.

How to Measure a Dinosaur

Children have intuitive ideas about measurement and enjoy testing their ideas. They will enjoy testing some of Most's measurement ideas with this activity.

1. Gather a variety of measuring tools (rulers, yardsticks, tape measure, meter sticks), clipboards, paper, and pencils.

2. Give each pair of children a clipboard stocked with paper and a pencil.

3. Take students on a walk to measure some of the things from *The Littlest Dinosaurs*, such as musical instruments, a refrigerator, a tall teacher, a cafeteria table, and playground equipment. Have students record information, listing the item and measurement.

4. Follow up by inviting students to compare and contrast the measurement of things they found on their walk with the things in Most's book. Are their measurements approximately the same? What might account for differences?

My Little Dinosaur Book

This mini-book gives students another opportunity to compare dinosaurs from *The Littlest Dinosaurs*.

1. Give each child a copy of the mini-book text boxes (page 52). Have children cut apart the text boxes and glue each to the top of a sheet of paper. Tell children to place the pages in order and staple them to make a book.

2. Revisit the book to review dinosaur names and sizes. Refer students to the chart (After Reading, Book Talk) for additional reference.

3. Invite students to fill in names and lengths of dinosaurs according to each page, and then make a comparison to something in the classroom. For example, on page 4, they may compare a lesothosaurus (four feet long) to a table in the classroom. Remind students to come up with their own comparisons, not the ones from the book. Provide measuring tools so that students can check their measurements before completing the sentences. Have students complete each page by drawing a picture of the dinosaur and the item they are comparing it to.

4. When the mini-books are complete, display them in the reading area so that students can discover new ways to compare dinosaurs to everyday objects.

String Measurements

Building a foundation of learning skills in measurement is important, and using nonstandard measurement is one of the ways children can do that.

1. Gather the following materials: string (a different length for each child) and assorted measuring tools (such as yardsticks, tape measures, rulers, and meter sticks).

2. Demonstrate the proper way to measure with a string, making sure the item is measured from end to end.

3. Give each child a string. Invite children to find something in the classroom that is about the same length as their string.

4. Once children have located something the same length as their string, have them choose a measuring tool and measure their string. On a sheet of paper, have students write the name and draw a picture of the item they measured and record the length. Have them attach the string to the bottom of the paper.

5. Bring students together to share their findings one at a time. As children share, have them remain standing, positioning themselves in order from shortest to longest measurement (or visa versa).

6. Finally, display papers in the same order to give children opportunities to revisit measurements and to provide a visual reference for making comparisons and estimates.

Measuring Munchies

Children will enjoy a nonstandard measurement activity that ends in a delicious and healthy snack. Be sure to check for food allergies before beginning.

1. Arrange pretzel rods, small crackers, slices of cheese, grapes, and carrot sticks on a tray and place them at a table.

2. Invite students to select some snacks. Then lead them in making comparisons before they enjoy their snack:

   - How many carrot sticks does it take to equal the length of one pretzel rod?

   - How many cheese slices does it take to equal the length of your longest snack? How does the way you turn the cheese slice change your answer?

   - If you wanted to measure the snack tray, which would make more sense to use: grapes or pretzel rods? Why?

Tip

Children naturally explore measurement concepts while building at the block center and playing in the dramatic play center. Use questions to draw out mathematical learning:

- Which one is longer? Shorter?

- How can you tell which block is heaviest? Lightest?

- Which container holds more/less? How do you know?

1
My Little Dinosaur Book

Name _____

Date _____

2
The littlest dinosaur was named

_____ .

This dinosaur

was _____ long.
    (measurement)

It was as long as

_____ .

3
The biggest dinosaur was named

_____ .

This dinosaur

was _____ long.
    (measurement)

It was as long as

_____ .

4
_____
    (dinosaur name)

was _____ long.
    (measurement)

It was as long as

_____ .

5
_____
    (dinosaur name)

was _____ long.
    (measurement)

It was as long as

_____ .

6
_____
    (dinosaur name)

was _____ long.
    (measurement)

It was as long as

_____ .

Is It Larger? Is It Smaller?

by Tana Hoban

❖❖

(GREENWILLOW BOOKS, 1985)

Vivid, thought-provoking photographs generate measurement questions of all sorts. Each page compares sizes and amounts of things through an artistic lens. The open-ended photographs are arranged creatively to get readers thinking about size and measurement. This wordless picture book speaks mathematically for itself!

Before Reading

Math Talk

Before reading, inform children that this book has no words but uses pictures to give readers information. Encourage children to look for the math meaning in each photograph, explaining that this book focuses on the size of different objects. Beginning with the cover, initiate math discussions based on the photographs, using comparative terms, such as "Which item in the photograph looks like it is the biggest? Which item looks the smallest?"

After Reading

Book Talk

Artfully illustrated wordless picture books are an area of literature that often leaves a lot of room for creative discussion. Use these prompts to encourage discussion that highlights how much children can learn from a book's illustrations:

◎ What did you notice about the photographs in this book?

◎ What is something you discovered by looking at the photographs in this book?

◎ What would you tell others they can learn if they read this book?

Meeting the Math Standards

Measurement

◆ Identifying length, weight, volume, and area

◆ Comparing and ordering objects using these characteristics

A Different Perspective

Invite children to use their measurement skills to compare items in the book's photographs. Have each child choose one photograph from the book and write about it, using comparison words such as *bigger, smaller,* and *taller.* Let children dictate as needed. Encourage children to consider what the photographer is trying to communicate through the photos.

Measure It!

This activity takes students beyond using words to compare objects and engages them in taking measurements in some innovative ways.

1. Invite students to bring in an object from home that they can easily measure. Provide objects for children to choose from if they don't have an object from home.

2. Display the objects and initiate a discussion about measuring them. Ask: "How could you measure these without using a ruler [yardstick, tape measure, meter stick, and so on]?" List ideas, such as a length of yarn, a stick, and a unit block.

3. Display the objects and some of the measuring tools from the list. Invite students to measure the items using any of the nonstandard measurement tools. Have them record their measurements, making sure to tell what they measured, the measuring tool they used, and the measurement.

4. Let children compare their answers to each object and discuss their results. Do any of the measurements vary from student to student? What are some possible explanations for this?

5. Ask students if they think their forms of nonstandard measurement worked. Encourage them to share their reasoning. Explain that we use a standard measuring system so that an object's measurement is consistent.

6. Have students take turns measuring the same items using a ruler or yardstick. Compare measurements, and then discuss any differences between standard measurements of the same object. Were the differences as great as those with the nonstandard tools?

Find the Size

The photographer put a lot of thought into setting up each scene to invite comparisons. Encourage students to create scenes of their own that invite comparisons about size and measurement.

1. Gather several different items of varying sizes and group them together, using photographs from *Is It Larger? Is It Smaller?* as a model.

2. Invite students to make observations that incorporate ideas related to size and measurement about the scene you set up—for example, they might say, "I notice that the red block is larger than the yellow bear."

3. Repeat with a few different arrangements of objects (anything will work—art supplies, math manipulatives, play dishes from the dramatic play area, or other objects from around the classroom).

4. Invite children to work in pairs and design their own scenes. Take photographs if possible for a class wordless picture book. Let children visit one another's arrangements and share observations that incorporate measurement words.

More, Fewer, Largest, Longest

It's important to use the language of math in daily conversations with children. For example, at calendar time, or when looking at groups of something, try posing these questions:

- What do you see more of?
- How many fewer does _____ have than _____ ?
- Which one has the fewest?
- Which one is the smallest [largest, longest, shortest, heaviest, lightest]?

Book Links

Children deepen their understanding of measurement concepts while enjoying these favorite stories:

Fannie in the Kitchen: The Whole Story From Soup to Nuts of How Fannie Farmer Invented Recipes With Precise Measurements
by Deborah Hopkinson
(Simon and Schuster, 2001)

Young Marcia is not happy to learn that a mother's helper named Fannie Farmer is coming to live with them. She has a change of heart when Fannie whips up the most delectable food she has ever tasted.

How Big Is a Foot?
by Rolf Myller
(Yearling, 1991)

When the King orders a bed built, confusion erupts about whose foot to use for the measurements: the King's or the carpenter's? So begins the emergence of the standard foot measurement.

Inch by Inch
by Leo Lionni
(HarperTrophy, 1995)

An inchworm measuring parts of birds introduces young readers to the concept of an inch.

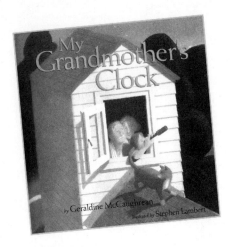

My Grandmother's Clock

by Geraldine McCaughrean

❖

(CLARION, 2002)

Meeting the Math Standards

Algebra

◆ Understanding qualitative change

Measurement

◆ Using clocks to tell time

◆ Using calendars to tell time

◆ Understanding the passage of time

Grandmother doesn't need a clock—she measures her hours by how long it takes Grandfather to read the newspaper, the minutes by how long it takes to put thoughts into words, and seconds by the beating of her heart.

Before Reading

Ask students to brainstorm ways that they know what time it is. For example, does the sun coming up tell them it's time to wake up? Does a bell tell them when the school day begins? Does the smell of something cooking tell them it's almost dinnertime? Do they have a bedtime? Who helps them know when it is this time? Discuss how clocks can help people know when it's time to do something, too. As you get ready to read, ask children to guess how the grandmother in the story knows what time it is. Then have them listen to find out.

After Reading

The story *My Grandmother's Clock* evokes feelings of comfort and safety as the little girl spends time with her grandparents. Invite students to make connections to the story by remembering places they love.

◎ Invite children to do a quick write (a sentence or two) or quick sketch about a place they love.

◎ Draw out language from students by asking them to recall how they felt when they spent time in this place. Have them name some of the reasons they felt the way they did.

◎ Guide children to recognize that, while their special places might not be the same as the girl's in the story, their feelings might be similar.

My Book About Time

This mini-book helps children develop common referents for time by guiding them to think about their day in terms of time frames.

1. Have students think about a typical day in their lives—for example, that school day. Discuss with children the things they can expect will happen in the day—such as calendar time, center time, read aloud, lunch, recess, and daily news.

2. Give each child four copies of the clock pattern (page 59). Copy the following text on chart paper and have children copy on their pages:

   Page 1 (cover): My Book About Time

                                 Name   Date

   Page 2:   In the morning I wake up at _____ o'clock.

   Page 3:   At school I _____ at _____ o'clock.

   Page 4:   At night I go to bed at _____ o'clock.

3. Have students complete pages 2–4 by filling in the blank(s) and drawing in the clock's hands to match their sentence. Children can draw hands on the cover to represent any time they like. Provide assistance as necessary with this step.

Monthly Calendars

These calendars reinforce the concept of how long a month is while giving children a beautiful project to take home and use.

1. Display a calendar of the current month. Discuss the organization of the calendar, including the way in which days and weeks are arranged and where the numbers begin and end and why.

2. Make a calendar template with five rows of seven squares each. Give each child a copy. Have children write the name of the month and fill in the correct dates, using the class calendar as reference.

3. Review special days that are coming up that month, including special school events and days that are special to children for other reasons (such as their birthdays). Have students mark these days on their calendar.

4. Have children fold a large sheet of construction paper in half and glue the reproducible calendar to the bottom half. Invite children to draw a picture that reflects the current month. Have them glue it to the top half of the paper (above the calendar).

5. Repeat this procedure at the beginning of each new month. Children can take home the calendars each month to display at home as a reminder to families of what's coming up.

Tip

Use a teaching clock with movable hands to show the different times students write in their mini-books. Let students revisit their books and use the clock to show different times.

What Can You Do in One Minute?

Children learn time in everyday routines and by talking about time with adults and other children. Concrete examples of time passing help children better understand the concept of time.

1. Show students a one-minute timer (hourglass style with sand) and explain how it works—the sand in the timer passes from the top to the bottom in one minute.

2. Turn over the timer to demonstrate how long one minute is. After one minute, invite students to share their perceptions: "Was one minute a long time? A short time?"

3. Generate a class list of things students think they can do in one minute. Depending on the age level of students, activities might include writing numbers from one to 25, singing the alphabet song, or answering ten addition problems.

4. As a class, use the timer to time yourselves doing different things. For example, how many jumping jacks can you do together in one minute? How many times can you toss a ball from student to student?

5. Invite students to share their perceptions after being active for one minute: "Does a minute seem longer when you sit quietly or when you are busy?"

Old Father Time

In this Old Maid–style card game, students learn to match analog time to digital time.

1. Have students pair up to play this game. Give each pair a set of playing cards (pages 60–61). Players cut apart the cards and color them if they wish.

2. Players shuffle the cards and deal them. (One player will have an extra card.) Children place any analog and digital clock matches in their hands faceup on the table.

3. Play begins with one player choosing a card from the second player's hand, hoping it will match a card in his or her own hand. If it does, that player places the match faceup on the table.

4. Players take turns in this manner, with each player trying to avoid being left with the "Old Father Time" card.

5. The game is over when all matches are made and one player is left holding the "Old Father Time" card.

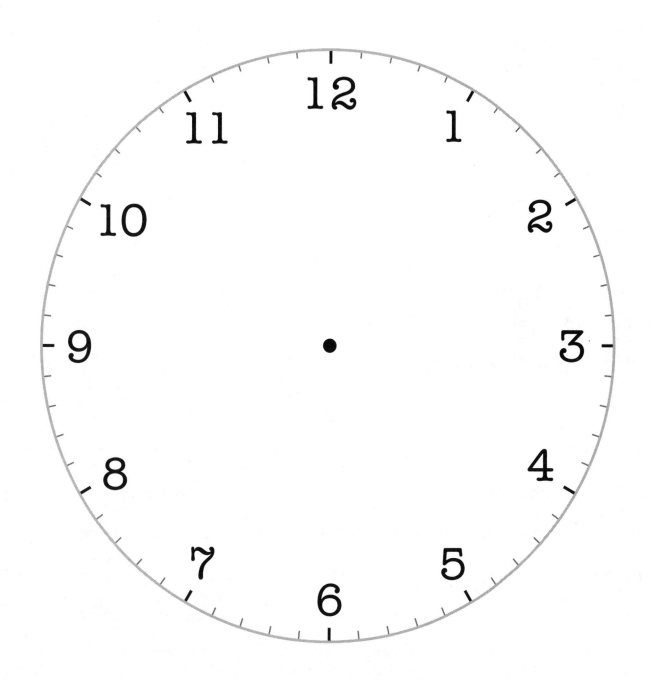

Old Father Time

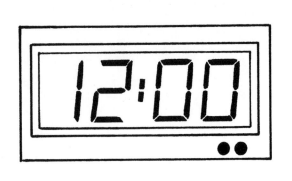

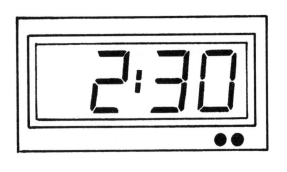

Teaching Early Math Skills With Favorite Picture Books © 2001 by Constance J. Leuenberger, Scholastic Teaching Resources

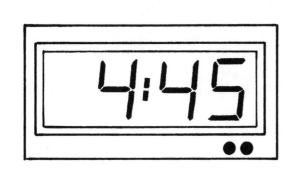

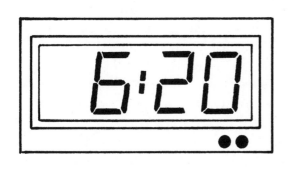

The Best Kind of Gift

by Kathi Appelt

❖❖

(HARPERCOLLINS, 2003)

Meeting the Math Standards

Measurement

◆ Understanding the attributes of volume and weight

◆ Understanding how to measure

◆ Using appropriate tools to measure

◆ Making estimates and comparisons of weight

Tip

▲▲▲▲▲▲

This text has the soft rolling sound of the southern vernacular, just begging to be read aloud. Invite students to make connections to ways they use expression (a component of fluency) when they read by inviting them to try out different voices as they recite lines from the story. For example, have them use a southern vernacular to read the first page of the story, beginning with "Yes, indeed!" Then have them read the same passage again with little inflection. Which made them feel like they were part of the story?

"**Yes, indeed! There is a brand-new parson at the Dogwood All-Faiths Tabernacle...**" begins this book. To celebrate the arrival of the new parson, the community decides to have a pounding. Little Jory Timmons doesn't know what a pounding is until his mother explains, "It's when everyone takes a pound o' this and a pound o' that to make Brother Harper feel at home." The remainder of the story follows Jory as he tries to find the perfect pound-sized gift.

Before Reading

Little Jory tries very hard to find the perfect gift for a pounding—a type of welcoming party where everyone brings a pound of something to greet new neighbors. Introduce children to this word and let them tell what they know about this unit of measurement. Ask students to think about the following question as they listen to the story: "Does every gift for the pounding equal a pound?"

After Reading

Use the question posed in Before Reading to guide a discussion that also strengthens children's ability to recall important details of a story.

◎ What are some of the gifts people in the community brought to the pounding? (a pie, a sack of corn, and so on)

◎ Which gifts for the pounding do you think really equal a pound? (Encourage children to explain their reasoning.)

◎ What are some other gifts that people might have brought to the pounding? (Encourage creative thinking, as well as attention to the concept of a pound.)

A Pound O' This and a Pound O' That

Children begin to understand attributes when they have opportunities for hands-on investigation. Use this experiment to encourage students to explore weight as an attribute of different objects.

1. Set up a center area with a scale and ten items for weighing. Some things that are easy for children to weigh are bags of beans or rice, unit blocks, boxes of crayons, cans of soup, fruit, and books. Place copies of the record sheet (below) at the center.

2. As children visit the center in pairs, have them estimate the weight of each item, weigh it, and record the weight on the record sheet.

3. Discuss children's findings. Encourage them to use measurement words to describe the weight of different objects—for example, "A can of soup is heavier than a box of crayons."

A Pound O' This and a Pound O' That

Name _____ Date _____

Item	Estimate	Actual Weight

Make It Equal

When Jory went to the pounding in the story *The Best Kind of Gift*, everyone brought something, but each gift didn't weigh exactly a pound. Sometimes, however, it is important to make sure that things are of equal weight. Try this activity to reinforce this concept.

1. Set up a center area with a balance scale and several items to measure, such as unit blocks, marbles, paper clips, shells, and rocks.

2. Invite children to compare the weight of different items. For example, a child might place some marbles on one side of the scale and then fill the other side with paper clips until it balances. Are there more marbles or paper clips? But do they weigh the same?

3. To further explore the concept of equal weight, have children write equation sentences for the items on the scales—for example, 3 marbles = 25 paper clips.

Book Links

The following books highlight measurement skills such as weight, mass, and proportion:

Biggest, Strongest, Fastest
by Steve Jenkins
(Houghton Mifflin, 1995)

This book combines amazing animal facts while comparing scale, proportion, and other attributes of animals.

Just a Little Bit
by Ann Tompert
(Houghton Mifflin, 1993)

When Mouse and Elephant try to balance on a seesaw, their animal friends come to the rescue to even out the load.

What's in Fox's Sack? An Old English Tale
by Paul Galdone
(Clarion, 1982)

This story helps emphasize the concept of mass when a sly fox with only a bee in his sack fools one villager after another into trading their goods.

Ordering Weight and Amount

Transitive reasoning relates to comparing one object to two others and making a judgment about the objects. This is a very challenging skill to master, and it requires a lot of hands-on practice. Here's one activity that invites students to compare objects and make these kinds of decisions.

1. Fill ten clear plastic bottles with different amounts of colored water in half-inch to one-inch increments. The bottles should range from nearly empty to full.

2. Replace the lids, making sure they are on tightly to avoid spills.

3. Invite children to place the bottles in order by estimating the weight and comparing the amount of liquid in each bottle. Ask questions relating to weight and amount, such as "Which one is heavier? Which one has more liquid? Which has the least amount of liquid? Which one is lightest? If you were going away for the day and wanted to take something to drink with you, which one do you think you would take? Why?"

Going to a Pounding!

Children make connections when they are encouraged to explore and experiment with a concept. Invite students to use what they've learned about weight and further explore the meaning of a pound with this activity.

1. Invite children to pretend they are going to a pounding and need to find a pound of something to bring with them. What might they bring?

2. Give each child a plastic grocery bag. Then let children go on a "pound hunt" without leaving the classroom. Invite students to fill their bags with items that they believe equal a pound.

3. Have children weigh their items to determine if what they found is less than, more than, or equal to a pound. Then have them take away or add items as necessary to make a pound.

Fall Leaves Fall

by Zoe Hall

❖

(SCHOLASTIC, 2000)

Two siblings frolic in the fall leaves, catching, stomping, kicking, collecting, and comparing the leaves. Of course, the big piles of raked leaves are also perfect for jumping into. Leaves from maple, sassafras, oak, gingko, and beech trees are featured in this colorful picture book. An illustration at the end explains how leaves grow throughout the year.

Meeting the Math Standards

Data Analysis
and Probability

◆ Gathering data about surroundings

◆ Sorting and classifying objects

◆ Organizing data

◆ Using graphs to represent data

◆ Describing data

Before Reading

Ask students if they have ever collected leaves (or something else) and sorted them. Invite students to tell about the different ways they can sort. Encourage students to think about these ways to sort as they enjoy the story.

After Reading

This fiction book has some nonfiction elements in it. Encourage children to think about the differences between fiction and nonfiction with these questions:

◎ Do you think this book is fiction or nonfiction? What are some clues?

◎ What parts of the story are from the author's imagination?

◎ What parts of the story give you factual information?

◎ In what ways are some other books you know similar to this book?

Tip

Invite children to glue one of their leaves on a sheet of paper and then write about it, as a scientist would, using detail about the color, type, size, and edges. Bind leaf descriptions together to make a class book about leaves.

Organizing Leaves

No matter the season, leaves make perfect sorting and graphing material.

1. Invite each child to bring in two or three leaves. Have extras on hand for children who are unable to bring in leaves.

2. As children share their leaves, notice the different kinds. Then have children combine their leaves in one pile. Ask: "How many leaves are in the pile? What is the dominant color of the leaves? What type of leaf edge is most common?" When students reply that it is difficult to see all the leaves in the pile, ask them to brainstorm ways they can arrange the leaves to see them more easily. Explain to students that data (leaves) must be displayed in an organized way to determine its characteristics.

3. Guide students in making a graph with the leaves, first deciding what characteristics to sort the leaves by—for example, by types of leaves (maple, oak, beech), leaf color, edges, or size. Explain that graphs are a way of sorting information to make it easier to analyze. Point out that graphs display one attribute of an item at a time.

4. Have students then take turns taping the leaves on a graph (set up on a large sheet of paper). For uniformity, have children first tape each leaf to a standard square of paper before adding it to the graph. Label the graph accordingly.

5. When the graph is complete, ask questions to bring out more math concepts: "Which leaf group has the most/fewest? Can you tell without counting? How? What does our graph tell you? How many more _____ leaves than _____ leaves? How can you tell? Is this graph easy to read? Why?" Encourage students to make true statements about the graph—for example, "This graph shows that we chose more toothed leaves than wavy" or "This graph shows that we did not find any lobed leaves."

Leaf Venn Diagrams

Children will love using this Venn diagram activity to sort leaves.

1. Enlarge and make copies of the leaf patterns (below). Give each child one leaf pattern. Review with students the different types of leaf edges (lobed, toothed, wavy, smooth). Invite them to determine which type they have.

2. Have students color their leaf with one of the following colors: brown, orange, red, yellow, green, purple.

3. When all the leaves are colored, gather children in a circle on the floor. In the center, overlap two yarn "circles" (tie lengths of yarn and stretch them to form circles) to create a Venn diagram.

4. Invite a volunteer to place his or her leaf in the overlapping area of the Venn diagram. Based on the leaf color and type, label the two circles accordingly. For example, if the child places an orange lobed leaf in the overlapping area, label one circle "Orange" and the other "Lobed." (The center is then "Orange-Lobed.")

5. Children who have an orange and/or lobed leaf then take turns adding their leaf to the Venn diagram, deciding where the leaf goes based on the characteristics displayed.

6. Once students have placed their leaves in the Venn diagram, discuss results. Ask: "Why does this leaf belong here? Why does this not belong here? What name would you give this group of leaves? How could you sort these leaves another way?" Then repeat with a new leaf.

Book Links

Use these titles to support students' explorations with leaves:

Fall Leaves
by Mary Packard
(Scholastic, 2000)

Readers are treated to a romp in fresh fall leaves, with educational games and cards at the back of the book.

Fall Leaves Change Colors
by Kathleen Weidner Zoehfeld
(Scholastic, 2002)

This simple explanation of photosynthesis also explains how leaves change colors.

Red Leaf, Yellow Leaf
by Lois Ehlert
(Harcourt Brace, 1991)

This book follows the life of a sugar maple tree through the eyes of a child, and includes an appendix of scientific tree information.

Tell Me Tree: All About Trees for Kids
by Gail Gibbons
(Little Brown, 2002)

Packed with scientific information, this book introduces parts of trees and their functions.

Lobed

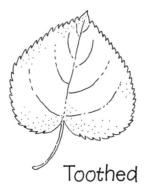

Toothed

Wavy

Smooth

Honey, I Love

by Eloise Greenfield

◆

(HARPERCOLLINS, 2002)

Meeting the Math Standards

Data Analysis and Probability

◆ Formulating questions

◆ Collecting, organizing, and displaying relevant data

◆ Gathering data

◆ Sorting and classifying based on attributes

◆ Representing data

◆ Describing data

◆ Making predictions and inferences

" I like the way he whistles and I like the way he walks. But honey, let me tell you that I LOVE the way he talks." This tender poem-turned–picture book about a child and the things she loves just begs to be read aloud. It may also inspire young readers to think about the things they love. Taking the book further, it serves as a springboard for class-generated lists and surveys on their favorite things, which makes for meaningful graphing activities.

Before Reading

The young narrator of *Honey, I Love* describes the things she loves, and one thing she doesn't (going to sleep!). Ask children if they think everyone loves the same things or different things. For example, do all kids love going in a sprinkler—a "flying pool" as the author calls it? Invite students to think of things they love as you read the book, and ways to find out the things others like or dislike.

After Reading

The cadence of this classic poem is mesmerizing. Explain that as readers, children will experience dialect in different stories and poems. Tell children that dialect is a particular way of talking that is used in certain regions of a country. Give examples of dialect they may have heard. Then explore further with these questions:

◎ Did the narrator choose the same words you would to describe things, or does she use language that is a little different?

◎ Why do you think the author chose to tell the story using a dialect?

◎ What is your favorite line from the story? (Then let children read it aloud to enjoy the poetic rhythm and share with the class.)

I Love a Flying Pool

"Honey, let me tell you that I LOVE a flying pool. I love to feel a flying pool . . ." Greenfield makes the language of this book so inviting. Use this language as a starting point for all kinds of graphing activities.

1. Based on the line above, generate a conversation with students about what their favorite warm weather activity is. List the activities and use them as categories for a bar graph.

2. Set up the graph accordingly. Have children make graph markers by drawing a picture of themselves (size the paper to the graph) doing their favorite of the activities listed.

3. Invite each child to vote for his or her favorite warm weather activity by placing the marker on the graph.

4. Use the bar graph to generate discussion. For example, ask: "How many more people like [activity] than [activity]? What would you say is the favorite of the activities on this graph? Why? If another class made a graph like this, do you think they would get the same results? Why?"

Morning Question

Children love to talk about their favorite things, and this engaging graphing activity will give them that opportunity while strengthening their math skills each morning.

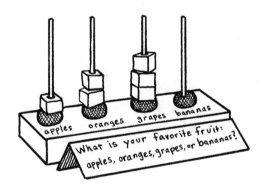

1. Place two to four lumps of play clay on a 12-inch-long unit block. Into each lump of clay insert a thin dowel. (The clay just holds the dowel in place.) The row of dowels will serve as a graph.

2. Generate some graphing questions based on students' likes and dislikes—for example, "What is your favorite fruit: apples, oranges, grapes, or bananas?" Write the questions on sentence strips.

3. Choose a question for the day and place the sentence strip next to the dowels. Place a label next to each dowel to indicate choices (such as Apples, Oranges, Grapes, Bananas). To answer the question, have children place an interlocking cube on the dowel. The dowel will fit through the hole in the cube, making the placement easy. The graph then becomes a representation of students' responses.

4. Use the graph during morning meeting or a math lesson as a source of discussion—for example, ask: "How many more people prefer apples than oranges? Do as many people prefer bananas as grapes?"

Tip

▲▲▲▲▲▲

As students become adept at understanding the nature of graph questions, let the helper of the day set up a graph question for use the next morning.

Tip

Young children can usually point out characteristics that are evident but have a hard time with the concept of something "not having" an attribute. When lining up children to leave the classroom, and at other transition times during the day, invite them to line up by attributes they do not have ("Everyone who is not wearing blue today line up").

Book Links

These books work well as springboards to sorting and graphing activities. Many of them also help generate questions for surveys:

Dave's Down-to-Earth Rock Shop
by Stuart J. Murphy
(HarperTrophy, 2000)

Each time Josh and Amy check the displays at Dave's Down-to-Earth Rock Shop, the rocks are organized and classified in a different way, first by size and then by more complex categories as the story continues.

Guess Who My Favorite Person Is
by Byrd Baylor
(Scribner, 1977)

The characters in this story trade information about their favorite things—from their favorite color to their favorite memory.

People
by Peter Spier
(Doubleday, 1980)

Explore a variety of cultures in a book that compares and contrasts the people of the world.

This One's Got It, This One Doesn't

Gather children together in a circle on the rug and play a thought-provoking game that focuses on sorting by attributes.

1. Choose two children to lead the game together. Quietly help the leaders decide on an attribute that they are going to use to sort a group of items, such as books (this attribute is kept a secret!).

2. The leaders pull out items in the group one at a time that have the chosen attribute (such as a picture of an animal on the cover).

3. When the leaders are finished selecting items, children try to determine what the attribute is. Repeat with new leaders and a new attribute (and new items if desired).

What's Your Favorite?

The narrator in the book certainly had a lot of favorites; hone students' interviewing and graphing skills with mini-books that invite them to share some favorites.

1. Before photocopying the mini-book (page 71–72), complete pages 2–4 by filling in the titles of five books the class has recently read. (Fill in the same titles on each page.)

2. Give each child a copy of the mini-book pages. Have children cut apart the pages, place them in order, and staple to bind.

3. On page 2 of the mini-book, invite students to check their favorite book and complete the sentence to tell why.

4. Next, have students interview five classmates, asking them about their favorite book. They can record responses as tallies.

5. Have students graph the data they collected (pages 2–3), then answer the questions to analyze it.

6. To extend students' learning, invite them to share their survey findings. Encourage discussion about the similarities and differences in the survey results. Pose questions, such as "Are any of our results the same? Different? Why? Who might be interested in using this information? Why?"

Favorite Books

Name _____ Date _____

①

Place a check next to your favorite book.

☐ _____
☐ _____
☐ _____
☐ _____
☐ _____

This is my favorite book because _____

_____.

②

What's Your Favorite?

Take a survey. Ask five classmates what their favorite books are.
Use tallies to record answers.

_____   _____

_____   _____

_____   _____

_____   _____

_____   _____

③

Graph your data from pages 2 and 3. Color in a box for each tally mark.

Number of People					
5					
4					
3					
2					
1					
0					

Title: ⬜ ⬜ ⬜ ⬜ ⬜

(Book Titles)

More people like _____ than _____.

Not as many people like _____ as

_____ or _____.

Write one more true statement about your graph: _____

_____.

④

Seven Blind Mice

by Ed Young

(PHILOMEL BOOKS, 1992)

This 1993 Caldecott Honor book tells the story of seven blind mice and their surprise at finding a "strange Something by their pond." Each mouse takes a turn, a day at a time beginning on Monday, to investigate the "strange Something." Upon returning, each mouse reports what the object is believed to be. Finally, on Sunday, White Mouse goes to investigate and explores the entire object, announcing that the "strange Something" is an elephant. At the end the author reveals the mouse moral: "Knowing in part may make a fine tale, but wisdom comes from seeing the whole."

Meeting the Math Standards

Data Analysis and Probability

◆ Gathering data about surroundings

◆ Describing data

◆ Making predictions and using probability

Before Reading

Math Talk

In this book, the mice were very eager to solve their problem, but they weren't considering all the information. Encourage students to listen to the story carefully and use the illustrations to help them determine what the "strange Something" is. Invite children to find other math concepts embedded in the book (counting and days of the week).

After Reading

Book Talk

Gathering data to make an informed decision is always important, whether in math or in everyday life. In this story, each mouse leaves with part but not all of the data. The last mouse teaches us that it's critical to assess the whole situation before coming to a conclusion.

◎ Why do you think each mouse explored only a part of the elephant?

◎ When did you first realize that the "strange Something" was an elephant? How likely was it that the creature was an elephant? Would it be likely for you to find an elephant where we live? Why or why not?

◎ What do you think of the mouse moral at the end of the story?

◎ Is it really important to see "the whole"? Why?

Tip

▲▲▲▲▲▲

To vary the activity, try the following scents: place a few coffee grounds under a cotton ball, a piece of dryer sheet cut up and hidden under a cotton ball, and garlic salt sprinkled on a cotton ball.

What Does It Feel Like?

When the mice were gathering data about the "strange Something," they relied on their sense of touch. For this activity, students will use only their sense of touch to try to understand *Seven Blind Mice* from the perspective of the mice.

1. Fill several lunch bags with different items that have varied surfaces and shapes—for example, sandpaper, cotton balls, satin ribbon, wool, and odd shaped things such as kitchen gadgets (check for safety). You'll want to include items that are soft, smooth, rough, fuzzy, prickly, and so on.

2. Gather children in a circle and pass around the bags (one at a time). Have children close their eyes, use their sense of touch to explore the contents, and think about what might be inside.

3. When all students have had the opportunity to investigate the contents of a bag, invite them to share information. Does this help them learn more about what's inside? (Reveal contents after students have had time to revise guesses.)

What's That Smell?

This activity works great at a science center to help children learn more about using all their senses to gather data.

1. Gather the following materials: five film canisters, cotton balls, cooking extracts (such as anise, lemon, cinnamon, orange, and almond).

2. Place a cotton ball in each canister. On each cotton ball, place a drop of cooking extract. Replace the tops on the canisters to preserve the smell. Number each canister and create a key for self-checking.

3. Give each child a copy of the record sheet (page 76). Invite students to lift the lid of each canister and guess what the smell is, then replace the lid and record their guesses.

It's Puzzling

At the end of *Seven Blind Mice*, the author reveals the mouse moral: "Knowing in part may make a fine tale, but wisdom comes from seeing the whole." To bring this idea home to students, try this puzzling activity.

1. Find a puzzle that students are unfamiliar with, and that has enough pieces for every child in the class to have at least one piece.

2. Give each child a puzzle piece (or two).

3. Invite students to study their puzzle piece, trying to determine what their piece is part of. Encourage discussion in this process.

4. Have students collaborate to find out whose puzzle pieces might fit together. For example, a couple of students might notice they each have what looks like part of a bird's wing.

5. Then have children put the puzzle together. Discuss the puzzle as a whole and how it compares to what they originally thought their piece might be. Explain that when scientists study things, they gather data and put it together piece by piece, like a puzzle.

Elephant Probability

How probable, or likely, is it that the mice found an elephant in the story? It could be very probable if the story was set in Africa, but the author doesn't tell us this. Probability is a tough concept for young children to understand. Use this activity, adapted from "Pottle's Probability" in *Meeting the Math Standards With Favorite Picture Books* by Bob Krech (Scholastic, 2002), to help scaffold their learning.

1. Make two copies of the elephant patterns, for a total of 30 elephants (page 76). Color 25 elephants gray and five pink. Cut out the elephants.

2. Discuss the concept of probability with students. Ask: "What does it mean if something is impossible? What does it mean if something is likely to happen? Unlikely to happen?"

3. Show students all the elephants, and then place them in a lunch sack. Ask students to predict which color elephant you will pull from the bag. Encourage students to explain their reasoning, using words from the discussion about probability—for example, "It's likely that the elephant will be gray. There is a greater probability, because there were more gray elephants than pink elephants."

4. Take an elephant from the bag and have children note the color (and whether they correctly predicted it).

5. Continue taking elephants from the bag one at a time, having children first predict the color. Encourage children to base their predictions on the colors of elephants in the bag, and on how many of each color you have already pulled out.

Book Links

These books highlight the importance of including all data when explaining or telling about something:

The Day Jimmy's Boas Ate the Wash
by Trinka Hakes Noble
(Dial, 1980)

A child recounts his field trip to the farm, from the most recent events to the first events.

The Important Book
by Margaret Wise Brown
(HarperCollins, 1949)

Attributes of familiar items are outlined, highlighting the most important attribute.

It Looked Like Spilt Milk
by Charles G. Shaw
(HarperCollins, 1947)

Clouds are silhouetted on each page, leaving children guessing: Is it a rabbit, a bird, or is it really just spilt milk?

Tip

▲▲▲▲▲▲

As a follow-up, have children try the same activity with a partner. Give partners a copy of the elephant patterns (page 76). Have them color and cut out the elephants, and then place them in a bag. Have partners take turns pulling out an elephant, first discussing the probability of its being gray or pink. Again, encourage children to base their predictions on the number of each color previously pulled out of the bag.

What's That Smell?

Name _____ Date _____

Canister Number	What I Think It Is	What It Really Is
①		
②		
③		
④		
⑤		

Elephant Probability

Chrysanthemum

by Kevin Henkes

❖❖❖

(GREENWILLOW BOOKS, 1991)

Chrysanthemum loved her name until she started school and the children teased her about the length of it. "It scarcely fits on your name tag," says classmate Rita at every opportunity. In the end Chrysanthemum is validated when a favorite music teacher names her newborn daughter Chrysanthemum.

Before Reading

Explain to students that this is a book about a little mouse girl who is teased about her name, Chrysanthemum. Some of the children think her name is too long. Before reading, make a graph on chart paper with the numbers 1 through 15 running along the top columns. Write the name "Chrysanthemum" in the blanks in the top row (one letter per cell), showing on the graph that Chrysanthemum has 13 letters in her name. Invite students to write their names on the graph (one letter to a cell) to display the number of letters in their names. Discuss the graph with questions, such as "Is Chrysanthemum the longest name on our graph? Which name is the shortest? How many names have more than five letters? How many names have four letters?"

After Reading

Each story has a problem; that's the element that keeps the reader wondering what is going to happen next. Chrysanthemum had a problem that many kids face at school: teasing. Discuss how this problem shaped the plot of the story.

◎ What was the problem in this story?

◎ How do you think Chrysanthemum could have solved her problem? What would you have done if you were Chrysanthemum?

◎ How do you think Chrysanthemum felt at the end of the book when Mrs. Twinkle revealed her name, and announced she was thinking of naming her baby Chrysanthemum? How do you think the other children felt?

Meeting the Math Standards

Data Analysis and Probability

◆ Gathering data about surroundings

◆ Representing data using graphs

◆ Describing data

◆ Making predictions and using probability

Tip

Place the clothespins in a basket, and display the ribbon graph at a center for students to revisit on their own. Be sure to save the clothespins for use with other graphing activities!

Ribbon Graph

Chrysanthemum's name was very long. Would it fit on a clothespin? Exploring this question helps children learn how to organize information.

1. Use a large strip of tagboard to make a graph. Write the numerals 2 through 14 (include more numbers if needed based on the length of students' names) along the bottom of the tagboard. Space the numbers evenly. From each numeral, hang a piece of string or ribbon to form a ribbon graph.

2. Give each student a spring-type clothespin. Have students write their name on the clothespin. Write the name Chrysanthemum on a clothespin, too.

3. Together, count the letters in the name Chrysanthemum. Model the activity by placing the clothespin on the graph, clipping it to the ribbon for 13. Invite children to bring their clothespins to the graph, clipping their clothespins to the ribbon that matches the number of letters in their name. For example, Cole would clip his clothespin to the ribbon for the numeral 4 to represent four letters in his name.

4. When each child has clipped a clothespin to the graph, ask questions to analyze the data—for example, "What is the most common number of letters in a name? The least common? What does this graph tell you?"

Rolling for Letters

This game focuses on probability and the number of letters in a child's name.

1. With two to four players, ask each player to write his or her name on a separate sheet of paper.

2. Have players take turns rolling two dice. (If you have students with more than 12 letters in their name, such as Chrysanthemum, you will need to use three dice.)

3. The player circles the letter of his or her name that corresponds to the total number rolled. For example, if Gavin rolled a two and a one, the total would be three, so he would circle the third letter in his name (*v*).

4. When all the letters in the names are circled, except the first one (you can't roll the number one with two dice), the game is over.

5. Discuss with students which numbers were more difficult to roll. Could anyone roll a one? Was a two difficult to roll? How about sixes, sevens, and eights? Explain that the combination of numbers on two dice has a lot to do with the odds of rolling each number. For example, the numbers six, seven, and eight have three possible combinations, making the probability greater for rolling these numbers. The numbers two, three, 11, and 12 have only one number combination for a set of two dice, making the probability of rolling these numbers less.

Guess Who!

This fun guessing game sorts kids by favorites.

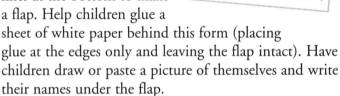

1. Give each child a copy of the form (page 80). Have children complete the form and cut along the dashed lines at the bottom to make a flap. Help children glue a sheet of white paper behind this form (placing glue at the edges only and leaving the flap intact). Have children draw or paste a picture of themselves and write their names under the flap.

2. Once children are finished, play a sorting game.

- Have all students stand.

- Without revealing the papers to students, begin reading from one—for example, "I like to play baseball." If this isn't something students like to do (and they didn't write it on their paper), then they sit down.

- Continue reading until only the child who wrote that paper is left standing.

- Repeat to feature each child.

Tip

The Guess Who activity is great for transition times, when you have one or two minutes before going to the next activity and you want to keep the class engaged. Keep these papers in a handy place, and read one each time you have an extra minute, until every child's has been read aloud.

Book Links

These books use graphs and probability to reinforce the concept of data analysis:

The Best Vacation Ever
by Stuart J. Murphy
(HarperCollins, 1997)

A young girl uses graphs, charts, and surveys to determine where her family should take a much-needed vacation, only to find that the best spot is their own backyard.

If You Give a Mouse a Cookie
by Laura Joffe Numeroff
(HarperCollins, 1985)

It's probable that once a little mouse has a cookie he's going to want some milk, and then a straw, and so on. This book reinforces the concepts of "likely" and "not likely."

Jumanji
by Chris Van Allsburg
(Houghton Mifflin, 1981)

This Caldecott winner takes the concepts of probability and chance to new levels, as two children play a game that their lives literally depend on.

Guess Who!

I like to _____ .

My favorite food is _____ .

My favorite color is _____ .

My favorite thing to do is _____ .

My favorite book is _____ .

Can you guess who I am?

Lift the flap to find out!

Teaching Early Math Skills With Favorite Picture Books © 2007 by Constance J. Leuenberger, Scholastic Teaching Resources